D0628174

Tips
for Using Your
Slow Cooker

Phyllis Pellman Good
and the friends of
Fix-It and Forget-It cookbooks

Intercourse, PA 17534
800/762-7171
www.GoodBooks.com

Acknowledgments

I feel like I've been surrounded by a circle of friends and neighbors while working on this book. Thank you, friends of the *Fix-It and Forget-It* cookbooks, for your tips and stories.

Thank you, Margaret, Tony, Cliff, and PJ, for all of your good work and imagination on this project. Merle and Kate, what would we do without your ideas?

—PPG

Illustrations throughout the book by Cheryl Benner
Design by Cliff Snyder

TIPS FOR USING YOUR SLOW COOKER
Copyright © 2012 by Good Books, Intercourse, PA 17534

International Standard Book Number: 978-1-56148-774-5
Library of Congress Control Number: 2012914616

The information in this book has been developed with care and accuracy and is presented in good faith. However, no warranty is given nor are results guaranteed. Neither the author nor the publisher has control over the materials or procedures used, and neither has any liability for any loss or damage related to the use of information contained in the book. Should any corrections be needed, they will be posted at www.GoodBooks.com. If a correction is not posted, please contact custserv@GoodBooks.com.

Publisher's Cataloging-in-Publication Data
Good, Phyllis Pellman.
    Tips for using your slow cooker / Phyllis Pellman Good and the friends of Fix-It and Forget It cookbooks.
        p. cm.
        ISBN 978-1-56148-774-5
        Includes index.

1. Electric cooking, Slow. 2. Cooking -- Equipment and supplies. I. Title.

TX827 G66 2013
641.5/884 --dc23   2012914616

Contents

A Handbook of True-Life Advice From Experienced Slow-Cooker Users!

Sure, there are the Owner's Manuals produced by slow cooker manufacturers.

- But do they tell you whether you need to brown meat before putting it into your slow cooker?

- Do they explain how to convert a stove-top or oven recipe so it can be cooked in a slow cooker?

- And how helpful are they when your lid breaks, or you have other small disasters?

Phyllis Pellman Good

Imagine a bunch of experienced slow-cooker users, sitting around the table, sharing their slow-cooker secrets and stories. That's what you've got in this collection.

You'll hear some conflicting ideas here—but then you can learn the pluses and minuses of having a divided crock, and whether to make your meal the night before or the morning of.

And don't miss the stories*—

- About slow-cooking in the car while driving to the campsite;
- About doing a monthly slow-cooker meal exchange with friends;
- About cooking breakfast for your over-night guests while you sleep in;
- About hosting stress-free holiday meals, wedding receptions, and Welcome-Home parties.

"I had a washer repairman, who had to make several visits to our house, comment on how good my house always smelled at supper-time as the slow cooker cooked away on the counter. My youngest son said the food always tastes that good, too, and invited the man to dinner!"

Julie Bazata

My sincere thanks to our faithful recipe contributors, and to the hundreds of thousands of followers of our Fix-It and Forget-It.com blog and our Facebook friends, for sharing your ingenuity and your matchless advice. Your real-life tested tips and discoveries** have made this book a handy resource for new and experienced slow-cooker cooks. You are the experts!

** *"We make hot damp towels with large smooth stones in our slow cooker— it's a home, hot-stone massage."*

Katherine Heldstab, Pittsburg, PA

Phyllis Pellman Good

Choosing a Slow Cooker

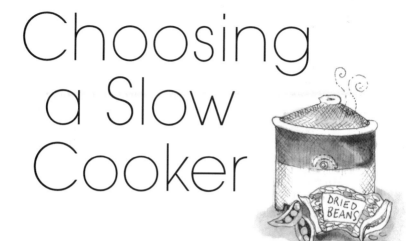

Features

1. I look for a removable crock. I used to have a 3-qt slow cooker that was all one piece and I had to worry whether or not I got the cord wet or water in the electrical unit.

Tamie Jamison, Kennewick, WA

2. My slow cooker has a seal with locks on the lid so it doesn't spill on the go. I love this feature.

Suzanne Steinbaecher, Lancaster, PA

3. I love a locking lid! It keeps little noses out of the slow cooker, and it's great for taking to a potluck. Also I like slow cookers to have a "warm" feature so I don't overcook food.

Nancy Wright, Decatur, AL

4. My next slow cooker needs to have the lock on the lid so I can carry soup in it for church meals.

Sara Dismore, Harrison, MI

5. I've noticed glass lids fit better than plastic ones, so I look for a slow cooker with a glass lid.

Arlene Hall, Houston, PA

6. Mine doesn't have a lid rest. I'd love if it had a piece that allowed me to just tilt the lid back. It seems like I always get too much water back into the crock when I lift the lid.

Amy Schultz, Lancaster, PA

7. I love that the newer slow cookers have more cooking settings to choose from, including just to hold the food on warm when it is done.

Sheila J. Moline, Reno, NV

8. I like the programmable slow cookers that go to warm automatically when the cooking time is done as I don't always get home at the same time.

Barbara Delcogliano, Colonie, NY

9. I love the auto high-to-low feature! It cooks on high for part of the time, then on low for the remainder.

Tracy Gossoo, Naples, NY

10. I do not like slow cookers with pre-set cooking hour times. I often use mine for times that are in-between the pre-set times.

Paula King, Wauseon, OH

11. I like the ones that are digital, have a removable base, and a place for steam to escape.

Tajuana Rhodes, Kansas City, MO

12. I have a programmable 6-quart model that has a locking lid so I can travel safely with it. It includes a large plastic serving spoon that snaps onto

the lid handle. I can set the slow cooker for time *or* temperature. It comes with a thermometer probe, and when the meat reaches the internal temperature which I have programmed into the unit, it switches to warm so as not to overcook the dish.

Karen Arn, Helena, AL

13. I love a retractable cord.
Jean Moulton, Windsor, ME

14. I wish I had the clip on the lid for the serving spoon. Mine are always on a small plate in front of the slow cooker and it looks messy.
Edward Engelman, Menasha, WI

15. I have a divided crock, and I don't like it because the smaller side cooks much faster and dries the food out.
Patty Bouteiller, Young Harris, GA

16. I'd love an insert that would enable me to cook two dishes in the same crock without having to buy yet another machine.
Julie Hamilton, Lititz, PA

We include tips from various viewpoints so you can make your own fully-informed decision. For example, some cooks love their divided crocks and some do not. Think of this book as a circle of cooks discussing their experiences and preferences. We hope you benefit from all of that as you decide how to proceed.

17. I have a divided crock in my slow cooker but the divider isn't removable. To me, it's not worth the expense since the foods have to be spooned out and they need to cook the same amount of time. I can accomplish more using 2 slow cookers!
Nancy Kelley, Orlando, FL

18. I have one cooker that has a divided crock so you can make two completely different dishes at the same time. Handy!
Kris Sloan, Centralia, WA

Accessories

1. I use a cake pan and a small trivet to raise meats or items I'm cooking and love them both!

Sandy Olson, Turton, SD

2. I trimmed a cookie rack to fit into my crock under my chicken to keep it raised from the grease.

Colleen Van Dyke, New Holstein, WI

3. A rack to cook meat out of the drippings is nice. I use my expandable vegetable steamer for that purpose now.

Martha Deaton, Fulton, MS

4. An accessory I wish I had for my slow cooker. . . Hmmmm — perhaps Brad Pitt to help me cook?

Gaille Robertson, Wheat Ridge, CO

Size and Shape

1. The most important consideration is the size. There is no reason to get a huge one if you are only going to be cooking for 1 or 2 people; that is how I got one of my slow cookers from my mother-in-law!

Rebecca Dumas

2. I knew I wanted a large slow cooker to cook whole chickens, ham shoulders, and turkey breasts. I have a smaller slow cooker just for vegetable dishes and side casseroles.

Donna Davis, Horse Cave, KY

3. I like a large slow cooker because I like to make a lot, and then I freeze it or share it.

Melissa LeClair, Frederick, MD

4. Purchase a large slow cooker, even if you have a small family. Oval-shaped slow cookers work well to accommodate roasts.

Cathy Fraser, Albuquerque, NM

5. I look for oblong cookers to allow room for

the baking insert (loaf pan) for breads and cakes, as well as long cuts of meat such as pork loin.

Melinda Myers, Mount Joy, PA

6. Over the years I have had several different types. I prefer oblong because meat cuts seem to fit better.

Tammy Fazenbaker, Baltimore, MD

7. I prefer oval so whole chickens fit better.

Tracy Gossoo, Naples, NY

The Case for Owning More Than One Slow Cooker

1. I wanted one to use when cooking at home for just my husband and me. I also wanted one large enough to take food to a big gathering or when hosting a group in my home. The shape doesn't really matter to me.

Sharon Yoder, Doylestown, PA

11

2. I have various sizes because most likely I won't need the same quantities of various foods. For instance, I use my largest one for a whole ham, and then the smallest to heat up and keep the gravy warm until serving time.

Sharon Miller, Holmesville, OH

3. I keep my extra slow cooker for baking potatoes because it doesn't have a removable crock. It's like having a portable oven.

Tess Vowels, Belle, MO

4. There are *so* many reasons for owning more than one slow cooker! I can double recipes. I can prepare a variety of appetizers for parties. I can enhance my party theme by having different types of slow cookers, such as my football cooker. I can prepare meals that require a more shallow crock in my oval shape, and I can prepare large meats in the oval also. My round, deeper crock cooks hotter, so I prepare foods in it that I want to cook up faster.

Rebecca Key, Boulder City, NV

5. I use two slow cookers for a typical dinner: one with a vegetarian recipe and one for my meat-eating husband.

Bernadette Smith, Hibbing, MN

6. I own more than one slow cooker so I can come home to a whole meal instead of just the main dish.

Delilah Swinford, Anderson, IN

7. I can do more than one dish at a time. I can pick the correct size for the recipe. I can let a friend borrow one and still have one at home to use!

Paula King, Wauseon, OH

8. Having a family of four, I have found that a 3-quart slow cooker is the ideal size. For 20 years I made many dinners with just one size. When the lid for my old 3-quart slow cooker broke, I found a 2½-quart which cost the same as an entire brand-new slow cooker, but the new lid also fit perfectly on my old 3-quart slow cooker, so I kept it. Then, when my neighbor cleaned out her closet, she gave me her 6-quart slow cooker.

Now that my husband and I have an empty nest, I bought a 2-quart slow cooker, the perfect size for just the two of us.

Recently, a friend of mine introduced me to an oval electric roaster which saves on energy costs. I was so impressed I got one for myself. After reading the instruction manual, I discovered it can also function as a slow cooker.

My family has grown to include in-laws and grandchildren. Thus the addition of a 17-quart roaster/slow cooker. My collection of slow cookers is now at six!

June S. Groff, Denver, PA

9. I do not use dividers in the slow cooker. However, with multiple slow cookers, I don't see as much of a need for a divider as I can just put something in the second slow cooker instead.

Noel Bigelow, Bellefontaine, OH

Other Considerations

1. Before buying a slow cooker, think ahead about the things you want to prepare in it.

   Tajuana Rhodes, Kansas City, MO

2. I own a pretty red slow cooker and it brightens up the table!

   Michele Rough, Mifflinville, PA

3. I asked for a slow cooker for Christmas a year ago, but my husband wanted to be sure it was an acceptable gift (afraid that buying me an appliance for a holiday would get him in trouble) so he checked with my best friend before buying it!

   Robyn Buck, Willow Street, PA

4. I suggest everyone should give slow cookers as wedding gifts. That's how I got my first one, and I fell in love. The husband is long gone but that slow cooker is still here!

   Suzanne Steinbaecher, Lancaster, PA

5. I gave slow cookers and slow-cooker cookbooks to my children for Christmas this year. They are busy with children and jobs, and I wanted them to have the chance to learn about how convenient slow cooking is.

   Deb Slater, Stilwell, KS

6. I pick slow cookers up at rummage sales when I see a size I don't have.

   Edward Engelman, Menasha, WI

7. If you ever break your lid, try going to the thrift store to find an old slow cooker that is the

same size. I made a cardboard template of the lid I needed so I knew what size I was looking for.

Rebecca Dumas

8. When using a slow cooker for the first time, keep an eye on it throughout the day to see how fast or slow it is cooking so adjustments can be made. Don't plug it in and forget it the first time you use it. I have a slow cooker from the 80's which cooks hotter than the newer cookers. It gets hot more quickly and cooks at a higher temperature. You learn as you go.

June S. Groff, Denver, PA

9. I wanted a slow cooker, but with so many choices out there, I could not commit. After several months of research, I finally chose a 6-quart oval slow cooker to handle large batches and cuts of meats. Our kids are small now, but I know someday they will be eating much more, and I will be able to make meals and freeze leftovers.

Karen Arn, Helena, AL

10. Fill your slow cooker with water and heat it on high for 1 hour. Use a thermometer to find the temperature of the water. It should be at 300° F, or whatever your owner's manual indicates.

Carol Eveleth, Wellman. IA

11. When I first got my slow cooker, I filled it with water and set it on low for 2 hours then checked the temp with a thermometer. I turned it to high for 2 more hours and checked it again. I like to test this every year just to see where I'm at.

Colleen Van Dyke, New Holstein, WI

12. I have multiple sclerosis and only have use of one hand. The simpler the preparation and cooking, the better, so I love my slow cooker. Using the cooking bags is a blessing to me because clean up is easier. I recommend slow cooking to people that have disabilities such as myself.

Bonnie Denny Schoeneman, Mantua, OH

Stories
About the
First Time

Beans

1. I bought a 2-quart Rival slow cooker and a Rival hard-bound cookbook. I put dried beans, seasoning and water in the slow cooker at bedtime, turned it on, and let the beans cook overnight. By lunchtime, they were all done and not overcooked. I never had to soak them or anything. I liked that since I didn't really have to be bothered with the soaking.

Nancy Kelley, Orlando, FL

2. I made chili. It was a disaster because I added salt to dry beans and they never got soft.

Therisa Wilson, Brownsville, OR

3. The first recipe was a pot of pinto beans and they turned out great. I had always cooked them on the stove and it would take all day. The slow cooker really did not reduce the time a great deal; but I didn't have to worry about them burning. It was amazing.

Sheila Diggs, Lubbock, TX

4. One Super Bowl Sunday my hubby invited all his friends over, but I was bushed from a long, hard, busy Saturday night at the restaurant I work at. I wondered what could I make for 20 people when I wasn't too happy to be cooking for a crowd again.

I made chili in my slow cooker. Then I made cornbread, corn salad, and brownies with other stuff I had on hand. My husband was stoked. Needless to say I got the rest I needed, and now it is a tradition.

Gayle Hall, Harbor, OR

Beef

1. I got everything ready to cook while we were away at church. Upon arriving home from church, I looked forward to walking in and smelling the mouth-watering smell of pot roast. We smelled nothing.

I forgot to plug it in.

Bonnie Denny Schoeneman, Mantua, OH

2. I had just begun to date my future husband. As he is an army reservist, his unit had to do their Annual Training which lasted 2 weeks.

Well, the night before he came home, I baked banana nut bread, browned a roast and cut up vegetables. I took my slow cooker to work that morning and proceeded to cook his roast in the break room at the clinic where I worked. The smell drove everyone, including the patients, crazy.

Needless to say he asked me to marry him 4 months after that and 17 years later, he still brags on my cooking.

Sally Skupien, Spring, TX

3. The first recipe I made in a slow cooker, which my boss gave me as a housewarming gift when I lived alone, was a Mexican-inspired steak stew. It was delicious!

Shelby Sill, Dallas, TX

4. I received my first slow cooker as a bridal shower gift in 1982. We were newly married and both busy working, so I made many meals in the slow cooker (and still do).

My first try was beef stew. I was pleasantly surprised at how tender the beef was cooked.

My mother-in-law told me to always buy a beef chuck roast for stew and to cut it up myself into chunks instead of spending more money at the grocery store to buy pre-cut stew meat. I still take her advice today.

Audrey Romonosky, Austin, TX

5. Unfortunately, my first slow cooker dish was a disastrous beef stew. I had never used a slow cooker before and had no idea that opening the lid and stirring every hour was a "no-no".

Tina Schwab, South Attleboro, MA

6. As a young married woman, I tried Irish stew first, but I overfilled the crock. The stew simmered over and down the sides and cooked the finish right off the metal surface! But the stew was delicious; I still make it regularly.

Amy Giannini, Zumbrota, MN

7. The first recipe I made was in 1982 for boeuf bourguignon. The recipe came with the slow cooker. It was absolutely fabulous.

Over the years I lost the recipe and have not found one as delicious to replace it. I am continuing my search.

Alys Corbin, Brick, NJ

8. I think my best recipe would be my first one which was a hamburger casserole. It calls for a lot of fresh foods, but when we were stationed in Okinawa, Japan, I could not get them as easily, so I was able to adapt the recipe to a canned version.

Melissa LeClair, Frederick, MD

9. My first slow cooker experience was as a young bride 30 years ago. I prepared a roast with one cup water and one package onion soup mix and went to work. I worried all day long about the house starting on fire.

When I got home, there was the most delicious roast ready to eat. I served it on buns with au jus. My husband thought it was the best meal ever.

Laurie Gunter, Woodbury, MN

10. About 20 years ago, I started a roast without enough liquid. When I got home from work, I saw how dry the roast looked and added some cold water. The crock shattered right in front of my eyes. I was so upset: I had not only ruined dinner, but also broken my slow cooker. Needless to say, we had pizza that night.

Julie Bazata

11. When I got married my mom bought me a slow cooker and taught me how to put a roast and veggies in it. She also told me that I should add a cup of fresh coffee to my slow cooker along with garlic, onion, and Worcestershire sauce. It makes the most tender delicious roast at the end of the day and no one knows that you put coffee in it.

Trina Mechling, Warren, OH

12. The first time I used my first slow cooker (I'm on my 5th now), I made beef stew. I was newly married and the cooker was one of my wedding presents.

I was completely nervous about leaving it on all day while we were at work, but of course everything was fine and we had a great dinner waiting for us at the end of a long day. I have been a convert (and a proselytizer) ever since.

Erika Muller, Merrick, NY

13. The first slow-cooker recipe I made was beef stew. It was a success. It tasted as good as my mother's recipe cooked in a pressure cooker. However, I cooked my stew while I was at work and my mother had to stay in the kitchen and oversee the pressure cooker on the stove!

Donna Sizemore, Hillsboro, OH

Chicken and Pork

1. We had just gotten married in August 1975, and my husband and mother-in-law had to teach me how to cook.

We were given a 3½-quart slow cooker that Christmas. I found a recipe in a woman's magazine for sliced sweet potatoes with pork chops layered on top and some orange juice and spices. It came out perfectly!

I still have that recipe somewhere amongst my cookbooks and piles of recipes.

Mary Ellen Stermer, Chemung, NY

2. I was a new bride and also a young and inexperienced cook when I invited my parents over for a pork roast cooked in my wedding gift slow cooker.

Well, I did follow a recipe, however, the recipe said 1 clove of garlic, and I thought it meant the whole head, so I used the whole thing! The roast was very garlicky!

Mary Vaughan, East Amherst, NY

3. The first thing I ever made in a slow cooker was pork chops with mushroom soup. It was so good, I wanted to roll in it.

Judy Sondergaard, Boulder City, NV

4. The first thing I made in a slow cooker was sauerkraut and smoked sausage with potatoes. My mom always made it in the oven, but I wanted to have it for supper one night after work and didn't want to have the oven on all day. I hoped it would work just as well in the slow cooker and it came out perfectly!

I learned through trial and error, though, to put the potatoes around the sides and put the meat in a well in the center, then cover all with kraut. Otherwise, the potatoes don't get done and the meat burns if it isn't covered.

Linda Knippen, Delphos, OH

5. The first time I cooked in a slow cooker wasn't with a recipe — I just started throwing stuff in the crock. Chopped chicken breast, cream of chicken soup, carrots, sweet potatoes, garlic, onion, parsley, black pepper, and gravy master. It was delicious!

Kris Riddervold, Ballston Spa, NY

Everything Else

1. I distinctly remember using a slow cooker to make hot dogs and sauerkraut in my college dorm room a long, long time ago. We weren't supposed to cook in our rooms.

When I got back from classes that afternoon, the entire floor smelled like hot dogs and sauerkraut and everyone was hungry!

Jill Brock, Rochester, NY

2. Up until I used my slow cooker, I had never really been able to cook. All I had the capability to do was heat up frozen foods.

Well, I decided to finally try my slow cooker that my husband and I got as a wedding present and cook him something besides frozen burritos. I found a simple roast recipe from a *Fix-It and Forget-It* book, and it came out great! I was so proud of myself, and my husband loved it.

Since then I have become a slow cooker genius, and my slow cooker pulled pork is a much requested item at potlucks. I have even gained the confidence to cook in the oven and on the stove as well.

Gabrielle Maag, Jefferson, LA

3. Years ago, we lived two hours away from the beach and would go often to spend the day, but when we went for a week, it was really special and fun. To make things better, a slow cooker was listed as part of the kitchen supplies. I was so excited to be able to use one for the first time! While we were on the beach, our pasta dinner was cooking.

It was a success and I rely on the slow cooker's convenience constantly now.

Sharon Garber, Mahwah, NJ

4. It was so long ago I can't remember what I cooked first, but it had to be a good experience because there is always a slow cooker on my counter. Always.

Elaine Flin, Chino, CA

5. I feel like a third generation slow-cooker chef. I can't remember what I made first!

When I was a girl, I remember helping my mom fill her slow cooker with spaghetti sauce and helping my grandmother fill hers with stew beef, onion, peppers and mushrooms. Watching them, I learned a bunch of easy, tasty recipes.

My first slow cooker was a hand-me-down from my mom, a 1970's avocado green one. I remember making meals for my roommates while going to graduate school in the 1990s. The meals cooked themselves while we had to study and we could make great food on a budget for our friends, too.

Lara Lupien, Waldoboro, ME

Don't Give Up!

1. Just do it. Just use it. Keep it handy and use it. Do *not* let it get shoved to the back of a cupboard. Your family will remember the good feelings that come from a comforting hot meal, served without the stress of last-minute cooking.

Kelley Millemon, Alton, IL

2. Try it on a day when you are home so you can monitor the slow cooker. Then, once you are comfortable with that recipe, you can set it to cook when you are gone.

Beth Moss, Clio, MI

3. It takes at least one meal to get the gist of your new slow cooker, so the first meal might not go perfectly. Have a back-up plan!

Maureen McCarthy, Framingham, MA

Cooking Efficiently

Prepping Ingredients

1. The slow cooker does force me to plan ahead for meals, but I love that once I prepare the meal in the slow cooker, I can pretty much "forget it."

I like to have cooked ground beef on hand in the freezer so that I can easily pull it out to make chili or spaghetti sauce in the slow cooker.

Addie Calvitt, Durham, NC

2. I prep a lot of veggies for soups once a month and throw them in the freezer. Then I can pour them in the crock, stir, turn it on, and I am off to work.

Amy Freeman Marquez, Brevard, NC

3. I try to plan my slow cooker use for the week. That way, if I know I will need onion for several dishes that week, I will cut onions for all of them at once. I will do the same for all my ingredients, just

prep everything for the week.

Then I separate ingredients into baggies and refrigerate or freeze them, depending on which day of the week they will be used; I call these "meal kits." I will grab one in the morning and toss it in the slow cooker and, with very little time and effort, we have a fabulous dinner ready that evening.

Since my family is all so involved in extra activities, it is hard to find time to cook a nutritious meal. When I use the slow cooker, we can just come home and eat and then we have very few dishes to wash.

Melanie Luce, Carrollton, TX

4. My friend takes the slow cooker liner bags and puts all the ingredients for a recipe in it, then ties it up and freezes it in a huge freezer bag.

When she is ready to cook it, she thaws it the night before and places it in the slow cooker in the morning. Her food is awesome!

Nicole Griffiths, Louisiana

5. I know a cook who browns enough ground beef for three meals during the week. She puts it all in the slow cooker overnight, scoops out the excess for later use, puts the rest of the ingredients together, and goes off to work.

Richard Dickson, Los Angeles, CA

6. I normally buy my ground beef in 5-lb packages, then I brown it in my Dutch oven with onions and garlic. Then after decanting off excess grease and cooling, I place 2-cup portions in freezer bags, flatten and squeeze out excess air and freeze.

Then when I use my slow cooker, I just drop that meat in the pot, add the other ingredients and go off on my day knowing that my meal is done when I get home!

Denise B. Stoeckel, Auburn, AL

7. I pre-make meatloaf when I buy meat, then freeze it. I pop in the meatloaf in the morning and it is done in a few hours. It is so very delicious because it keeps all of the moisture inside. The slow cooker makes it feel like I am not even cooking!

Michele Rough, Mifflinville, PA

8. When I don't feel like frying out ground meat for later use, I put 5 lbs. in my slow cooker with seasoning and beef broth. I can use cheaper ground beef because the broth highlights the flavor. I let my slow cooker do the cooking for me.

Then I pour off the grease and package the cooked ground beef in 1-lb serving sizes for the freezer. I use it to make spaghetti, sloppy joes, etc.

Randi Kubit, Strongsville, OH

9. My sister likes to buy her veggies at the salad bar at the local grocery store so they are already cut up and ready to use. Also, she only has to buy what she needs.

Jeanne Gibson, Ferguson, MO

10. In a slow cooker, you do not have to pre-soak dried beans before you cook with them, which is a real time-saver and step-saver in recipes.

Janet Peterson, Pierz, MN

11. I soak dry beans in my slow cooker overnight. In the morning, I rinse them, add more water and turn it on.

Becky Price, Dallas, PA

12. Here is something I found out: when beans are soaked overnight, they absorb 1 cup of water per 1 cup of beans.

So, if you forget to soak your beans, you can compensate by adding an extra cup of water per cup of beans and cooking on high for longer to make up for not soaking.

Rebekah Meyer, Caldwell, ID

13. My biggest time saver is shopping at the big box stores to keep my pantry well stocked. I keep multiple bags of boneless skinless chicken breasts and thighs, beef cuts and pork chops/loins in the freezer. I also buy large bags of frozen stir-fry veggies and single veggies like broccoli and baby carrots.

In my pantry are diced tomatoes, sliced mushrooms, canned veggies of all types, canned soups, seasonings, chicken and beef broth, and onion soup mix.

I also buy those little 4-packs of red and white wines since we are not wine drinkers and I hate to open a whole bottle and then have it go to waste.

So now I know that when I'm searching my *Fix-It and Forget-It* cookbooks and find something I want to make, I'll probably have the ingredients.

Becky Thompson, San Antonio, TX

14. If a recipe calls for a spice mix, I double or even quadruple the amounts and store it in a covered container so that I don't have to do it the next time I make this recipe. Don't forget to label the container!

Patricia Slattery, Hopewell Junction, NY

15. Make sure your ingredients are of equal sizes for even cooking.

Judy Faro, Dallas, GA

16. If you like mush, cut veggies and others finely; otherwise, we prefer veggies cut larger so there is texture when the cooking is done.

Jan Mast, Lancaster, PA

17. I turn the empty slow cooker on while I'm prepping ingredients. That way it is nice and warm when I put the food in it.

Michelle Clement, Elk Grove, CA

The Case for Browning Meat First

1. About browning meat, my simple guideline used to be—if I have time, and the inclination to wash another pan, I'll do it. If I don't, I won't.

But then I realized that if I browned the meat before putting it into the slow cooker, the meat cooked off a lot of its fat in the process. I could drain the meat and then put it into the cooker, saving the people I'm cooking for a lot of calories.

Most times these days, I brown the meat.

Phyllis Pellman Good, Lancaster, PA

2. I don't always brown chicken before using it in the slow cooker, but I do brown beef. It simply adds a lot of flavor to the dish.

Tina Campbell, Lancaster, PA

3. I always flour, season and sear my meat before putting it in the slow cooker. I reserve the drippings for the whatever liquid I am using—it makes a huge difference in the flavor of the dish.

Nancy Looby, Hometown, IL

4. Add a small amount of water to the pan in which you browned the meat. When the pan is scraped clean and the water is brown, pour it into the slow cooker for added flavor.

Deb Ward, Oxford, CT

5. Particularly with chicken, it doesn't look

as anemic if it's browned first. It's more or less aesthetics for me. Just lightly browning chops or chicken gives them a much better appearance.

Molly Garza, Katy, TX

6. Browning makes beautiful brown, not gray, meat.

Patty Paulsen, South Jordan, UT

7. My husband hates boiled meat, but if he knows I browned it first, he will eat anything I make in the slow cooker.

Delilah Swinford, Anderson, IN

8. I brown my pork ribs in the broiler first before putting them in the slow cooker. It cooks off some of the fat.

Audrey Romonosky, Austin, TX

9. I usually brown the meat in olive oil. I dredge it in flour first as it makes a gravy when cooked.

Jean Robinson, Pemberton, NJ

10. When I brown, which I call searing, I season the meat and have a hot pan on the stove ready to sear in the juices of the meat. I have my slow cooker already set to low so it's warm when the meat is placed in it.

After searing, I will then add stock or wine to the pan to get the browned bits and then add the liquid and bits to the slow cooker.

Melody Rauscher, Wantage, NJ

11. I like to smear creamed horseradish on my pot roast before I sear it for extra low-fat flavor.

Celine Buck, Ft. Worth, TX

12. Trim off excess fat before browning. I like the flavor that the fat adds, and sometimes put the trimmings in the skillet, but not the slow cooker. I get a skillet *hot* — we are searing, not cooking to get it done. I use a good set of tongs to turn the meat without burning myself. I brown all sides/surfaces, and then put the meat in the slow cooker.

Barbara A. Elliott, Osawtomie, KS

13. When I'm short on time in the morning, I brown the meat the night before, and keep it in fridge.

Jill Bishop, Wallingford, CT

14. For food safety reasons, I always cook any ground meat first before putting it into the slow cooker, but I brown it in the microwave and rarely on the stove.

I put my ground meat into a strainer or colander and put the strainer or colander into a larger bowl. Microwave the meat while breaking it up and stirring it around every minute or so until all is cooked through.

You are also removing the fat by using this method of cooking ground meats.

Deb Slater, Stilwell, KS

15. I brown my meat first to caramelize the outside of the meat and create a flavor the slow cooker can't.

Suzanne Steinbaecher, Lancaster, PA

We include tips from various viewpoints so you can make your own fully-informed decision. For example, some cooks brown meat and some do not. Think of this book as a circle of cooks, discussing their experiences and preferences. We hope you benefit from all of that as you decide how to proceed.

The Case Against Browning First

1. I only cook with the leanest ground meats, and get no grease from them, so even if I don't precook the meat, I am not adding grease to my food.

Plus, I think that ground meats cooked in liquid

are more tender, and keep more of the natural meat flavors and juices.

Donna Davis, Horse Cave, KY

2. I don't brown meat before putting it in the slow cooker. It satisfies my desire to be lazy.

Susan Johnson, Minneapolis, MN

3. It's faster not to brown the meat. I have trouble getting my head around the idea of cooking the parts of a recipe before cooking it in a slow cooker. If I'm going to cook everything on the stove, why not just eat it then?

Beth Goering Tanner, Wichita, KS

4. If the meat is going in a sauce such as tomato, I don't bother. Otherwise, it does look more appetizing if it's browned first.

Mary Irish, Des Moines, IA

5. It depends on what I am cooking. I always brown ground beef and roasts, but not stew meat. I

also do not brown if we are barbecuing some meat.

Teresa Bennett, Newport, TN

6. Browning adds some color, but then there's one more pan to wash.

Beth Bigler, Lancaster, PA

7. I leave chicken raw when I put it in the slow cooker, and I think that makes the dish more moist. I also leave roasts and pork chops raw and they turn out more tender, in my opinion.

Maura Flick, Orlando, FL

8. I don't think anything is lost by not browning meat first. I believe it is actually more tender than if you were to brown it.

Marsha Kaanta, Escondido, CA

Preparing the Recipe in the Morning

1. Using a slow cooker saves busy people that frantic "what's for dinner?" rush at the end of the day. Five minutes or so in the morning will have a delightful meal on the table for your hungry family in the evening with no stress.

Angel Barnes, Kinderhook, IL

2. As a nurse, I worked the night shift for years. Nothing better than coming home, throwing supper in the slow cooker, going to bed and having dinner ready when you wake up! I never had enough left to freeze a meal ahead.

Sandy Olson, Turton, SD

3. For me, it works best to put together my slow cooker recipe the morning of. That saves messing up any storage dishes — the recipe can be made right into the slow cooker.

I hesitate to put it into the ceramic crock and refrigerate it, for fear of cracking the crock when I put it in the electrical unit to cook. I know of several people who do that, but some of their crocks have hair-line cracks all through them.

Sharon Miller, Holmesville, OH

4. I get everything prepared in the morning and I am free to do other tasks in my day, knowing that there is a nutritious dinner waiting for my family.

Also, clean up is during the day, instead of all the pots and pans waiting after supper for me when I'm tired.

Sheryl Gudgeon, Chambersburg, PA

5. I have Parkinson's disease and I have the most energy in the morning. I found that making my meals in the morning and using the slow cooker is a great benefit. It's nice to have it all prepared so that I can rest, as that is greatly needed in the late afternoon.

Emajoe Abeln, Cordova, TN

6. I put the slow cooker out at night before I go to bed to help remind me to prepare it in the morning, and then in the morning, I put everything inside and I'm off to work.

Kaye Mills, St. Peter, MN

Preparing the Recipe the Night Before

1. I normally put together my slow cooker dish before I clean up the dinner dishes. That way, I only have to clean the kitchen one time. The completed dish stays in the fridge overnight, covered in plastic wrap, and goes into the electrical unit in the morning.

Becky Thompson, San Antonio, TX

2. After a party at my house one night, several friends spent the night. So before I went to bed, I threw some fruits and oats into the slow cooker to make a breakfast cobbler. I made a sign and stood it in front of the cooker that said "Good Morning! Help yourself."

My friends got a delicious breakfast, and didn't have to wake up early to cook.

Deanna Wright, Leechburg, PA

3. My husband makes his apple butter in the slow cooker all night, then gets up the next morning and puts it in jars before work.

Kris Ross, Lake Worth, FL

4. I find it easier to prepare my slow cooker recipe the night before. If I am missing an ingredient, I can make the run to the store.

Colleen Van Dyke, New Holstein, WI

5. The morning of is when I actually assemble the recipe, but I try to group my ingredients the night before so I don't have to hunt for items or find I am missing something.

Charissa McCollum, Whitewright, TX

6. When I'm cooking meat that may result in a lot of fat or grease, I like to cook it overnight, then refrigerate it during the day. When I'm ready to fix dinner, I remove the solidified fat off the top of the dish, and reheat it. Much better!

Kris Sloan, Centralia, WA

7. I put the prepared crock in the refrigerator and get up during the night to plug it in depending on the time of day I need it.

Janet Peterson, Pierz, MN

Preparing Recipes and Food Ahead of Time

1. I will often make entire meals in the slow cooker, and then separate them into individually-sized containers, to make our own "freezer meals."

These are convenient to take to work and throw in the microwave. Or, with just the two of us, when we're not in the mood to have the same thing at the same time, we can have totally different dishes for dinner.

Josie-Lynn Belmont, Woodbine, GA

2. I cook everything in big batches and freeze it to have another time.

Even though we are now retired, we always have something on hand to eat and there is less time spent cooking.

Beverly Ronquillo, Marrero, LA

3. I make stock in the slow cooker using chicken bones/carcasses, veggies, herbs and spices, lots of garlic, and water. Then I freeze it for later use in other recipes.

Janie Lindsay, Silver Lake, OH

4. My favorite make-ahead-and-freeze slow cooker recipe is called King Ranch Chicken. The King Ranch used to cover most of south Texas and this dish originated from the Mexican ranch hands. It consists of layers of corn tortillas, shredded seasoned chicken, cheddar cheese, and cream of chicken soup with green chilis. Think of it like a chicken enchilada lasagna.

I make it ahead and let it firm in the fridge. Then I cut it into serving- size portions and freeze it in disposable lunch containers. It's an easy grab for the lunch box on the way out the door to work.

Becky Thompson, San Antonio, TX

5. I cook white beans and ham, then I put them in the freezer in small freezer cups, just enough for a meal. I remove the lid and put the cup in the microwave for a quick and easy meal, and I really enjoy them.

Nancy Peace, Kensett, AR

6. My girlfriends and I get together for dinner once a month. We each bring along with us 4 frozen slow cooker dinners, each for 6 people. Then we exchange our dinners, and each person goes home with 4 different dinners. It has been so much fun trying each other's recipes.

Melanie Miller, Flemington, NJ

7. Even with only two in the household now, I still make a huge cooker full of soup or stew. Thank goodness for a freezer so as to store future meals. I never call them leftovers!

Jean Robinson, Pemberton, NJ

8. For an instant quick lunch or dinner on busy days, I take an ice cream scoop to scoop individual servings of taco ground beef onto a wax-paper lined baking sheet, which then I freeze. When frozen, I place the individual servings in a freezer baggie.

Kristeen Bazan, Middleville, MI

9. I buy larger cuts of meat and cook them and break them down to portions and freeze them that way all the time. We have a vacuum sealer for that exact reason.

I've cooked beef, chicken, goat, lamb and pork in slow cookers and frozen all of them for future use with great success.

Alexis Roy, Sauk Rapids, MN

10. I have used my slow cooker to render lard. It melts well without being watched and I never worry about scorching. Then I cool it and put in containers to freeze.

Neva Mathes, Pella, IA

11. There was a sale on meat at the grocery store. So I did 2 slow

cookers of pulled barbecue pork for sandwiches and 2 slow cookers full of chicken quarters. I put the meat in on low before I went to bed, and when I got up in the morning, ta-dah! all 16 pounds of the meat was done. Plus, I had chicken broth to use for soup, too.

Christine Pietsch, Grimes, IA

12. We make a meat shopping trip to a large grocery store. When we get home, we make a big batch of meatballs and put them in the slow cooker with sauce and let them cook while we package the rest of the meat. We do the same thing with ropes of fresh Italian sausage and sauce in another slow cooker. We have meatball and sausage sandwiches for dinner and pack the rest up for the freezer.

Cindy Carl, Barto, PA

13. I will use my extra-large slow cooker for two roasts. I add extra broth for more juice.

After cooking, I shred one roast and put the

meat away in serving size containers, adding equal portions of remaining juice. Then I freeze the containers of shredded meat and broth. The kids can thaw a package for after school snack on a bun.

Laurie Gunter, Woodbury, MN

14. We freeze half of everything we make. This was really helpful after I had surgery last year. All my husband had to do at the end of the day was pull something out, thaw and reheat.

Ambriel Mccathern, Austin, TX

15. Cooking big batches of food once a week or maybe twice a month and freezing it up in portions is a real time saver. The rest of the week all I have to do is thaw it out.

Not only does it save time, but I make sure I have healthful meals available so I'm not tempted to head down to the local fast food emporium for something deep fried or loaded with sugar.

Gaille Robertson, Wheat Ridge, CO

16. I use my slow cooker to cook dry beans so they are ready to use in chili, burritos, baked beans, etc. I put the dry beans in the slow cooker the night before, fill cooker with water, and cook on low all night.

I also like to put chicken in the slow cooker to cook on low overnight so I have cooked chicken for my chicken dishes. Use plenty of water as the broth is so delicious, too.

Another good thing is to put 3 pounds or more of hamburger in the slow cooker and cook it. Just drain the meat and crumble—no stirring necessary while cooking!

Carol Eveleth, Wellman. IA

17. I will cook a lot of meat and use it throughout the week for different menu items.

For example, I throw frozen chicken breasts in the slow cooker. I shred them when they're cooked. One night we have chicken on top of salad, another night chicken salad sandwiches, and then, finally, tacos.

Shawna Rowan, Saint Marys, GA

18. Every year on the day before Thanksgiving, I peel and cube potatoes and put them in the slow cooker crock covered with water and set the crock in the fridge. In the morning I pull it out and plug it in. My potatoes cook perfectly. Then I drain, mash and return them to the crock to keep warm.

This is my favorite slow cooker trick because I hate standing over a hot stove at the last minute, boiling potatoes on Thanksgiving Day.

Julie Hamilton, Lititz, PA

19. For Thanksgiving, I always use a slow cooker for mashed potatoes that I cook and mash the

night before. In the morning, I take them out of the fridge and put them on warm until dinner.

And I also use four other slow cookers: for yams, pumpkin pie, hot fudge pudding cake and wassail.

Colleen Larson, Plain City, UT

20. When I buy boneless, skinless chicken breasts at a good price, I throw some in my big slow cooker with some broth and cook them on low overnight.

In the morning, I take them out and let them cool a bit, then put them in my Kitchen Aid stand mixer and it shreds the chicken perfectly. I freeze it in bags and it is so handy for recipes in the slow cooker or oven.

Julie Hamilton, Lititz, PA

21. I often thaw a whole package of chicken breasts and use two slow cookers simultaneously to cook each half in two completely different styles, the second batch to use for another meal later in the week. A great time saver!

For instance, I'll use the first batch for a chicken and rice meal that same evening, and the second I'll spice up for chicken burritos, fajitas, or enchiladas later in the week.

Sheryl Rogener, Tracy, CA

22. I love to use my slow cooker to cook any kind of dried beans. I buy organic in bulk and have very yummy beans with bean stock leftover.

I just put beans in the cooker, add enough water to cover by 2 inches, a swirl of olive oil, and one bay leaf. I quarter an onion and throw that in. I cover the crock and put it on high for 4 hours and my beans are perfect and ready to go.

Plus, once I strain it, the juice leftover is a very yummy broth or stock that can be used or frozen for soups or to mix in hummus, etc.

Amy Schultz, Lancaster, PA

23. I have a tradition of taking one day per week to cook for the entire day. I prepare meals ahead of time to create a supply of healthy food for when I

am in a hurry. On these occasions I often use 4 slow cookers at time.

At the end of the day, I am always pleased with the nutritious food that I find when I open all the lids. The aroma in the kitchen is amazing!

Virginia Rose Hartman, Akron, PA

Keeping Food From Sticking

1. The plastic slow cooker liners are a godsend. They make an easy slow-cooked meal even easier.

I will hand wash my crock every other week or so with warm soapy water, as sometimes the liners do leak.

Noel Bigelow, Bellefontaine, OH

2. I use a plastic liner, as I want my slow cooker to stay pretty for years.

Joy Goade Zowie, Beeville, TX

3. I use plastic liner bags if I am cooking with cheese. Otherwise I spray with cooking spray.

Linda E. Wilcox, Blythewood, SC

We include tips from various viewpoints so you can make your own fully-informed decision. For example, cooks keep food from sticking in different ways. Think of this book as a circle of cooks, discussing their experiences and preferences. We hope you benefit from all of that as you decide how to proceed.

4. I really like using the slow cooker bags, especially for roasts. I just take the roast out with a meat fork and then snip the end of the bag to strain the juices into a saucepan so I can thicken it to make a gravy.

Cindy Carl, Barto, PA

5. I have always used cooking spray. Just this week I tried one of the plastic liner bags for the first time. I liked it, and loved the clean up. However, the cost of the bags will prohibit me from using them frequently.

Kelley Millemon, Alton, IL

6. Slow cooker bags do make easy clean up, but on the other hand, the bags tend to fold over and food gets trapped in the folds so it is hard to get it all out. Also, the bags can tear.

Melanie Luce, Carrollton, TX

7. I've never greased, sprayed or used a plastic liner in my slow cooker —never had a problem with food sticking.

Ursula Prada, Edgartown, MA

8. I never worry about greasing my slow cooker because I can use an SOS pad to clean it up. Easy-peasy.

Katrina Pawlaczyk, Jackson, MI

9. I haven't found that sticking food is a problem in my slow cooker.
I most likely will not use a plastic liner because I don't like to heat food in plastic. I may grease the inside if necessary.

Gloria Lehman, Singers Glen, VA

10. I always use cooking spray instead of plastic liners. I'm not a fan of disposable items. I would rather wash my slow cooker with a little extra elbow grease than throw something away after one use.

Tina Schwab, South Attleboro, MA

11. I think the best thing you can do so the food doesn't stick is to make sure your crock has a good intact shiny glaze. When food starts sticking badly, it's time to get a new crock.

Elaine S. Good, Tiskilwa, IL

Cooking with the Lid Off

1. I slightly skew the top if I don't want too much liquid to build up, especially for the last couple of hours. Do that if you want your spaghetti sauce to reduce down and get thicker. Do it, too, if you are roasting meat and want some of the broth that has gathered to cook off.

Beth Moss, Clio, MI

2. I cook with the lid off when I want to thicken what is cooking or need to keep the collected lid moisture from dropping back into the cooker into the food. The lid does keep heat in the crock, so for thickening the recipe I usually have to turn it on high and stir periodically.

Deb Slater, Stilwell, KS

Reheating Food

1. If the food I want to reheat has been refrigerated, I put it on low for 2 or 3 hours.

If it is frozen soup or stew, I put it on low for 4 or 5 hours.

If it has cheese or milk ingredients, I usually just turn it to warm and let it go for a few hours, checking it every hour until it's ready.

Deanna Wright, Leechburg, PA

2. I reheat food in my slow cooker for about two hours on low.

Lori Holbrook, Blountville, TN

3. I reheat foods on low for probably 4 hours, stirring and testing along the way.

Christine Ranallo, Medina, NY

4. I like heating up soups or meats like roast or chicken in my slow cooker, but I don't like reheating pasta or rice dishes.

Rebecca Dumas

5. Chili, soups, and stews are all better the next day, so I do them the day before, then reheat the next day.

Jeramy Lawrence, Aurora, CO

6. I personally like my food to warm slowly and thoroughly, so I start it on high for about an hour then on low for a couple of hours after that. I stir it every thirty minutes or so.

Joetta Russell, Catoosa, OK

7. Soups, lentils and chilis are the easiest to reheat and usually taste even better when you have cooked them twice.

Brisja Riggins, Dorado, Puerto Rico

8. I have stacked Indian-style stainless cooking containers inside with different foods in each. This works fairly well for dahl and some meat dishes. It also works for reheating rice.

Elaine S. Good, Tiskilwa, IL

9. We have many fish fries and I use the slow cooker to keep the fish warm after they are cooked. This keeps them like fresh-cooked filets.

Norma Grieser, Sebring, FL

10. On low, I melt honey that has turned granular. It needs to be heated just slightly so as not to kill the good bacteria, but just enough to return the honey to its liquid state.

Jackie, Louisiana

11. I have a dinner plate that fits nicely over my slow cooker like a lid. When my husband is not ready to eat at the same time, I put water on high in the slow cooker and put the plate covered in foil on top to keep the plate and food warm until he is ready to eat.

Randi Kubit, Strongsville, OH

The Warm Setting

1. The warm setting is great for when dinner is ready, but your family isn't.
   Cindy Quinlan, Salinas, CA

2. I do not use the warm setting for more than 1 hour.
   Sydney Carter, Venice, FL

3. A couple of hours on the warm setting is pushing it. I'd say not more than two hours.
   Teresa Bennett, Newport, TN

4. I use the warm setting to just keep things like fondue warm without cooking them.
   Michelle Clement, Elk Grove, CA

5. Warm does not mean ignore; you still have to monitor and stir the food, checking for needed liquid.
   Marie McFadden, Clover, SC

6. The warm setting is great for when you want to keep the meal warm without really cooking longer. Or, to use for adding those last minute add-ins that you don't want to really cook, just heat a little, such as cream, cheese, garlic, and minute rice.
   Bonnie Anderson, Simpsonville, SC

7. After taking kabobs off the grill, I stand them upright in the slow cooker to keep warm with tented foil.
   Joyce Wing, Dixon, IL

8. I have used the warm setting on my slow cooker to keep hamburgers warm when cooking them for a large crowd. It is also good for warming taco shells for a crowd.

Martha Deaton, Fulton, MS

9. Holding mashed potatoes on the warm setting for 2-4 hours is okay, but only if the crock is full.

Patty Paulsen, South Jordan, UT

10. The warm setting is excellent for keeping gravies warm. If the

recipe has been cooking for several hours and it is done before the meal time, the warm setting keeps it from overcooking.

Sharon Miller, Holmesville, OH

Handling Leftovers

1. I use my slow cooker to turn leftovers into new meals by adding sauce or gravy. I also freeze leftover soups or chilis for quick meals on busy nights; add a grilled cheese sandwich or salad and supper is done.

Julie Bazata

2. I make most meals with an eye to using leftovers for lunches. We reheat most of what I make in the slow cooker.

Jill Brock, Rochester, NY

45

3. I freeze the leftovers from pot roast for beef and vegetable soup.

Katrina Pawlaczyk, Jackson, MI

4. When we have chili, I will store the left-overs in bowls in the freezer for my son to take with him for lunches. The frozen bowls of chili act as ice packs as well as lunch.

Colleen Van Dyke, New Holstein, WI

5. After the roast is finished from supper, I will put the leftovers back in the crock then into the refrigerator. They next day, I will add brown gravy and water with an onion and plug it in for roast beef sandwiches for supper.

Colleen Van Dyke, New Holstein, WI

6. Instead of halving a recipe, I prefer to make the whole amount and eat it several days, or take the leftovers to share with my son or mother.

Barbara Gautcher, Harrisonburg, VA

7. I cook a whole chicken on Sunday, and we have roast chicken and veggies for dinner. Leftovers are diced up for salads for lunch during the work week and chicken noodle soup for supper.

Regina Martin, Brownstown, PA

8. My favorite day to use my slow cooker is the day after Christmas, which is also my birthday. For Christmas, I make a full turkey dinner, but I make sure to make extra stuffing, mashed potatoes, and gravy. After we eat, the leftovers go straight into my slow cooker in this order: potatoes, stuffing, turkey, and gravy. Then I just put my crock in the fridge.

The next day all I have to do is plug it in. No cooking for my birthday! Plus, it cuts down on the number of containers to hold the leftovers.

Then I can go out and find any good after-Christmas sales while my birthday dinner heats up.

Tress Hewitt, Torrance, CA

9. Ice box glop is what we call it. We use all the good leftovers in the fridge and make a pot of mixed stew. On low in the slow cooker, it melds real well. We always have a pot of rice ready to pour it over.

Corliss Lewis, Cisco, TX

10. I like what I call dump soup. I either have beef broth or chicken broth, add spices and then add leftovers that are in the fridge.

Ronda Hall, Great Falls, MT

Relief for Busy Schedules

1. You can cook really healthy in a slow cooker, and it's ready when you arrive home from work. With the activity level of most families, I don't know why *more* people don't use them! You will spend less money if you cook in a slow cooker than you will on a fast food meal, and it's *real* food.

Mary Vaughan, East Amherst, NY

2. I can serve a hot healthy meal on a very busy day. If I have to take my kids to a dentist or doctor's appointment after school, I plan a slow cooker supper. That way when we get home, supper is ready and we can avoid the easier and less healthy option of running through the drive-thru.

Tina Schwab, South Attleboro, MA

3. I did a roasted chicken with vegetables and a peach cobbler for Sunday dinner. It was so nice to walk in the house after church and have it smell so delicious. It was even nicer knowing all I had to do was pop the rolls in the oven and change my clothes.

Sally Skupien, Spring, TX

4. My slow cookers help me feed my kids healthy meals while we juggle our busy schedules plus I save money since we don't have to hit the drive-thru like so many of my friends. As a busy, single mom, my slow cookers save me time, money and added calories.

Melanie Luce, Carrollton, TX

5. I made dinner in the slow cooker for a sick friend as well as enough for my family's dinner at the same time. Very efficient!

Allison Evans, Allen, TX

6. I can remember as a child, my grandmother and other community ladies gathering in the fall to make apple butter. It was an all-day affair: building fires, using those huge special pots, and stirring all day. There were always so many jars when we were done.

With a slow cooker, you can make just a few jars for gifts or immediate use and it doesn't tie you up all day. So easy!

Melissa Kinnaird, Gallipolis Ferry, WV

7. Chili is a big favorite in our home. If unexpected company stops by, we just add noodles or spoon it over baked potatoes. Hospitality on a budget is a wonderful thing for a single, working mom!

Colleen Van Dyke, New Holstein, WI

8. Because I have more than one slow cooker, I can crank out a whole meal without tending to it — my work schedule is very busy right now. I don't have to watch the clock or tend the kitchen. A slow cooker's timing forgiveness so I don't ruin the meal is the best benefit for me.

Patricia Soper, Holly Springs, NC

9. My time is valuable to me and I cherish the time I gain by setting and forgetting what I am cooking without having to come back and check for boil overs, burning pots, or stirring. A slow cooker helps me avoid all that.

Judy Faro, Dallas, GA

10. The foods in the slow cooker can generally "wait" until the remainder of the meal is done — a big plus.

Sharon Garber, Mahwah, NJ

11. I like to make a chicken and curry meal for our college grandchildren and their friends for Sunday dinner after church. I can easily cook rice while getting the rest of the foods and drinks on the table. It's delicious, ready quickly, and very nutritious.

Arianne Hochstetler, Goshen, IN

12. I use my slow cooker most often when I have guests. It's helpful to prepare the main dish and then concentrate on the rest of the meal. I don't feel pressured, so I'm able to relax and enjoy relating to the friends we are entertaining.

Arianne Hochstetler, Goshen, IN

13. I plan on slow cooker soups, casseroles or baked beans at least once per week. This allows me to plan anything outside the house while the meal is cooking: trips to town, shopping, appointments, etc.

Jean Moulton, Windsor, ME

14. I started using my slow cooker a lot when my second child was born. Around the time my husband was coming home from work, I was just frantic! The baby needed to eat, our older daughter was hungry and tired and just wanted Mommy, I was trying to get dinner on the table — usually whatever was fast and easy because that's all I had time for!

Once I started using my slow cooker, it just made things so much easier. I bought 2 books from the *Fix-It and Forget-It* series, so I had some good tried-and-true recipes to start with.

I could do all my meal prep earlier in the day, so the kitchen was also tidier. I had time to sit down and feed the baby, maybe even read a book to my daughter while the baby ate. Plus, I didn't have the pressure of tending something on the stove that might burn or boil over if I stepped away too long.

Suddenly I had some "wiggle-room" for when dinner would be ready, so I wasn't as stressed about possibly ruining our meal. The entire atmosphere of our home became more relaxed in the evenings, and my husband was much happier to come home to a wife and kids who were not frazzled and agitated.

Tress Hewitt, Torrance, CA

15. I often put together a slow cooker meal while my son eats his lunch. We can chat while I cook and then get back to his school work. A slow cooker is a great friend to a home schooling mother!

Brisja Riggins, Dorado, Puerto Rico

16. I have 4 children ages 17, 15, 8 and 10 months. I am always running someone somewhere. Using a slow cooker ensures dinner is always hot and ready for everyone no matter what time they are walking in the door.

Suzanne Steinbaecher, Lancaster, PA

Additional Tips

1. There's a trick to lifting a slow cooker lid.

Because a lot of moisture collects on the underside of your slow cooker's lid, tilt it quickly away from the food when you lift it off. Otherwise, you'll be diluting what you've carefully prepared in your slow cooker.

Phyllis Pellman Good, Lancaster, PA

2. If you have to remove the lid, be sure and wipe dry the rim of the pot before replacing the lid or the condensation will keep it from sitting tight.

Nancy Thackston, Gadsden, AL

3. I always give the side a quick touch a few minutes after turning the slow cooker on just to make sure it is really on and plugged in.

There have been several times I have come home and it is plugged in, but not turned on, or turned on and not plugged in. My husband just shakes his head and laughs. But the quick touch has saved me from this issue on several occasions.

Jennifer McClain, Hughesville, PA

4. I place my slow cookers on the kitchen counter in order of the meal: gravy near mashed potatoes, etc.

Jeanne Caia, Ontario, NY

5. I have found that cooking the rice at the very top of the slow cooker away from the bottom heating element helps keep it from burning or getting over cooked. I also make sure to put stuffing on the very top of the slow cooker when cooking that with the rest of the meal.

Noel Bigelow, Bellefontaine, OH

6. While using the slow cooker, I do not use the stove. So I will put a cutting board on the cold stovetop and put the slow cookers on the cutting board. That way there is more room for me on the counter top.

Jim Black, Farmington, NH

7. If I'm slow cooking at home, I place the slow cooker over a large stove burner because the stove can handle the heat from the cooker. Also, it's not in the way there as I am used to pots on the stove. This method frees up the counter for other uses.

Sandy Olson, Turton, SD

8. Don't put your slow cooker in the busiest part of your kitchen.

Hannah Deter, Grants Pass, OR

9. For some crazy reason, slow-cooker manu-facturers are often very secretive about the size of the slow cookers they make. That priceless bit of information tends to be only on the box. So use a permanent marker to write the size onto the bottom of the heating unit.

I mention this because you often don't know how full the quantity of food you're about to mix up will make your slow cooker.

Phyllis Pellman Good, Lancaster, PA

10. Always check the harder veggies with a fork one hour before the earliest time that the recipe says they are done. If the recipe says 8-10 hours on low, I check it at 7 hours.

Nancy Eaton, Manchester, CT

11. I have always pre-ferred to cook a roast, pork or beef, in the slow cooker. In the slow cooker, it comes out so ten-der that you can eat it with a spoon. When I am cook-ing for children or elderly persons, that can be quite an advantage!

Angel Barnes, Kinderhook, IL

12. I've heard of people cooking veggies in a slow cooker to make home-made baby food.

Jessica Czapla, Chicago, IL

13. I can use less expen-sive, and often less tender, cuts of meat in the slow cooker and have them come out as juicy and deli-cious as more expensive cuts.

Angel Barnes, Kinderhook, IL

14. I love making fresh yogurt in my slow cooker. It's pretty much no fuss and turns out great. It is so much better than any store-bought yogurt, and I know exactly what went into it.

Plus, my sons can add in fruit or nuts or chocolate in the morning or for a snack.

Trina Mechling, Warren, OH

15. You don't have to use pre-packaged mixes and canned soups in your slow cooker. Yes, they are time-savers, but they are expensive and full of possibly harmful additives.

I've been able to find lots of healthier ways to add flavor to my slow cooker recipes: herbs, balsamic vinegar, soy sauce, gourmet salts, citrus juices, and garlic, to name a few.

Sarah Herr, Goshen, IN

16. I use my slow cooker more in the summer months because it adds far less heat to my kitchen than the stove or oven. It also uses far less energy, which helps reduce my utility bills.

Angel Barnes, Kinderhook, IL

17. I have a temperature gun and it is the best. I can keep an eye on my food without disturbing it.

Amy Fields, Bumpass, VA

18. Plan ahead: they are called slow cookers for a reason. If you forgot to thaw something for dinner, it's time to use the microwave, not the slow cooker!

Nancy Kelley, Orlando, FL

19. I sometimes make a barrier by placing foil on top of the meat in the slow cooker and placing potatoes on the foil to keep the potatoes from cooking in the juice.

June S. Groff, Denver, PA

20. I made an entire meal in one slow cooker. I put chicken on the bottom with some Italian dressing coating the chicken. Then I put some sliced potatoes with pats of butter and salt and pepper in a packet of foil on top of the chicken. Then I used frozen mini corn cobs in foil with pats of butter around the outer edge. My family loved it.

Kathie High, Lititz, PA

21. I "bake" potatoes or sweet potatoes in my slow cooker. They do not have to be wrapped in aluminum foil, but I do if I want to cook them along with the meat for a meal that I'm cooking in the slow cooker.

Sometimes I cook carrots and potatoes with the meat in the slow cooker, but if I want the potatoes not to soak up meat juices, and be more like "baked" potatoes, I wrap them in foil before I put them in.

Martha Deaton, Fulton, MS

22. I have made a whole meal in the slow cooker with different dishes.

I make layers of food that I don't want mixed, each in its own foil layer, stacked using balls of crumpled foil to separate layers.

Karen Schulz, Janesville, WI

23. I have used a foil-package method, where you wrap different foods in foil packages. It makes a whole meal; you add different packages at different times depending what cooking times they need.

It works, but it takes away the beauty of using the slow cooker so you can be away all day and still have a delicious meal waiting for you. It did make clean up easy, though.

Betty Detweiler, Centreville, MI

24. Occasionally, I only have one slow cooker at my disposal, such as when I am helping someone at their home. I have made both the entree and the side dish at the same time by placing the ingredients for each dish into separate slow cooker liner bags.

Cathy Fraser, Albuquerque, NM

25. Sometimes my slow cooker dishes are hard to recreate because I open the pantry doors and just toss in what I happen to have on hand.

Patty Paulsen, South Jordan, UT

26. I just always keep trying new recipes and new ideas. I have a few favorite recipes, but every month I try to make a couple new slow cooker recipes so I don't get bored with the same old meals from my slow cooker.

Noel Bigelow, Bellefontaine, OH

27. Never leave a hungry husband and kids home alone with a slow cooker. Too many taste tests can cause a depletion in the final outcome of the recipe!

Deb Ward, Oxford, CT

28. Always add love to your dish. Do this by thinking lovingly of the people you will be serving the food to.

Kelley Millemon, Alton, IL

Cooking For Crowds

Planning Menus

1. Always make something that you have made before so you don't have any surprises.
   Frances Raabe, Seattle, WA

2. Make your menu carefully so that it is something a lot of people like or you will have a lot of waste.
   Tammi Anderson, Port Huron, MI

3. I plan comfort food for big groups; nothing too fussy.
   Jacinthe Fish, Barre, VT

4. Test your recipe before the event. Allow plenty of time for recipes to completely cook if they are for a larger amount than you normally make. I discovered that it can take quite a bit longer for some recipes to cook when the amounts are doubled or tripled.
   Sharon Yoder, Doylestown, PA

5. Make sure at least one of the meals is vegetarian.
   John Bradford, Saint Charles, IL

6. When making food for large groups, it is easier to make two crocks of the same recipe than it is to use a bigger roaster oven with its cooked-on crust to clean up. The food looks so much better in a slow cooker, and clean-up is so much easier. Easy makes happy!

Colleen Van Dyke, New Holstein, WI

7. I use several slow cookers at graduation parties. Everybody tends to get burned out on the usual cold salads and such in the summer, so using a slow cooker makes my parties stand out. It's where the good food is served!

Kristeen Bazan, Middleville, MI

8. When I have multiple cookers going for a group event, I lay dinner rolls, which I have put into baggies, on top of the lids of the slow cookers. I open the bag a bit so the rolls don't become soggy from steam build-up, and then I have nicely warmed rolls by serving time.

Betty Detweiler, Centreville, MI

9. For my bridal shower, we did a taco bar. We had four slow cookers: beef, chicken, refried beans, and nacho cheese.

Everyone was able to customize their own taco, everything that needed to be hot was, and everyone loved the idea!

Ashley Watkinson, Chesapeake, VA

10. On holidays, use your slow cookers for the side dishes and save the oven for the big item — like the Thanksgiving turkey.

I've never found a side dish that I couldn't cook in my slow cooker, plus slow cookers keep all those side dishes warm.

Cathy Hoyt, Moyock, NC

11. If the meal is served over a period of time, I stagger the food to cook over a period of time.

The last time I did this I was serving baked beans at an event where I fed 235 people sponsored by a county organization. I don't want mushy beans, so some pots were started later. By the last hour of the four hours we served, they were perfect.

Betty Detweiler, Centreville, MI

12. I only make one other hot food besides what is in the slow cooker.

I recently used the slow cooker for a Hanukkah party. It was a casual family party, so on my kitchen island I put out the slow cooker, rolls for sandwiches, a potato kugel out of the oven, and a salad. It was very little work for me as hostess, and everyone enjoyed the meal.

Natalia Armoza, Gardiner, NY

13. My family eats a lot of Mexican food, and my kids often request it for their birthday parties. I can make a big pot of beans in my slow cooker and then just do rice and taco meat on the stove. It makes a large meal for a reasonable price!

Tress Hewitt, Torrance, CA

14. For big holiday gatherings, my mom uses two large slow-cookers for soups. She adds a make-your-own sandwich section, a pickle tray, and a big bowl of chips. We all bring cookies and there's a great meal! Easy, make-ahead and fast clean-up.

Lara Lupien, Waldoboro, ME

Buffets

1. I prefer to use big slow cookers instead of chafing dishes with sterno cans and all the other food warmer items available. Just turn the slow cooker on the warm setting. Nothing sticks or burns, and because the inserts are so big, refills aren't required nearly as often, allowing me to spend more time with guests.

Joy York, Wildwood, GA

2. Sometimes warm is too warm, so I check the food once in a while. In a buffet, as the food

diminishes, what is left tends to overcook. I turn the slow cooker off if I need to.
Patty Paulsen, South Jordan, UT

3. Plug the slow cooker into the orange heavy-duty electrical cords and use a power strip for multiple outlets.
Sharon Garber, Mahwah, NJ

4. I tend to elevate my slow cookers on a box or cake stand on a buffet table. It cautions people that the cooker is hot. Also, people tend not to reach over the slow cooker then, so there's no chance of burns.
Adra Chim, Royse City, TX

5. Allow enough room on the table or counter for a place to set the lid down. It's hard to serve food onto a plate when you have a lid in your hand.
Too many lids get broken without a place for them.
Sandy Olson, Turton, SD

6. I put a tray on the buffet with a towel neatly folded on it for the slow cooker lid when people are serving themselves. This way, water droplets do not wreck the food with moisture or stain the buffet.
Joyce Wing, Dixon, IL

7. We hosted a Halloween costume party at our house for all our relatives, their kids and the kids' friends. Needless to say, I didn't want to be stuck in the kitchen, so we decided on a soup buffet for the menu. It was a hit! We had four different soups in four different slow cookers, and people went back to sample all four.

Angela Smith, Glenwood City, WI

8. On Thanksgiving, I use my slow cooker trio buffet with 3 pots going. Each one is set on separate temperatures so that the food in each is kept warm or hot, depending on what it is: hot gravy, warm rolls, hot veggie, etc.

Everyone has a nice plate of food that is the right temperature, even for seconds or thirds!

Judy Faro, Dallas, GA

9. If I am using a slow cooker to serve soups/casseroles as a buffet at a large function, I take the food in a sealed container separate from the slow cooker to avoid spills on the way.

If time is short at the event, I warm up the soup on the stovetop and then place it in the slow cooker —it makes serving quicker and the food is hotter.

Sharon Garber, Mahwah, NJ

Labeling Food & Slow Cookers

1. Make a sign that asks guests not to open the slow cooker and tells them what the food is. That way guests don't continue to open your lid, and they can easily find the recipe online if they have the name.

Kathryn Wesling, San Jose, CA

card next to the slow cooker for guests' information.

Kathleen Felmey, Gresham, OR

4. I wrote my name on the bottom of my slow cooker with permanent marker and it's still there after repeated washings.

Ellen Stier, Oceano, CA

5. Make a list of the cooker, its contents, and what time it will be complete. I like to be creative with it and name my cookers. People name their cars, so why can't we name our slow cookers! "Trixy will be done at 4:30pm and Roxann will be done at 5:15pm. . . ."

Melinda Myers, Mount Joy, PA

2. Make a tent out of an index card to label the food inside the cooker.

Becky Farley, Rio Rancho, NM

3. To be courteous for those with food sensitivities or allergies, place a list of ingredients on a 3x5

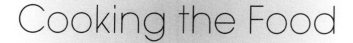

Cooking the Food

1. I always time things backward, starting with when I need to have everything done, and time backward for when to start

each item. This way everything is done at the same time and ready to serve.

Angela Smith, Glenwood City, WI

2. I keep a little notepad of when I started each slow cooker and how long I want to cook what's in each one. That way, I am not guessing throughout the day which one is ready and which one isn't.

Joni Redlinger, Keota, IA

3. Once the slow cookers are filled and cooking, enjoy yourself. Spend time with your guests and family while the slow cookers do the work. Make it *look* like you're busy cooking so you get all the praise.

Michael Feight, Eau Claire, WI

4. Cooking overnight is my friend when I'm cooking for groups. I have a ton of other things to do for special events, so I like to cook early.

Becky Thompson, San Antonio, TX

5. Take the slow cookers you're planning on using and fill them halfway with water and actually try plugging them in where you intend to use them and see how the electrical circuits hold up. Leave them on for several hours so you don't get a false sense of security.

Also, realize that it's a lot harder to handle a slow cooker filled with hot food. If you can cook it where you're going to serve it, all the better!

Alexis Roy, Sauk Rapids, Minnesota

6. Always use a GFCI outlet (an outlet with a reset button which is grounded to prevent electrical shocks) and if possible, put multiple slow cookers on separate circuits.

If that is not an option, always use a power strip with a breaker.

Jeanne Gibson, Ferguson, MO

7. Don't overfill the cooker just because the crowd is big. If you need to prepare more of the same dish, use multiple slow cookers.

Nancy Kelley, Orlando, FL

8. If you are doubling a slow cooker recipe for a large crowd, make sure to allow for a longer cooking time. I would recommend to start cooking

your doubled-up meal the night before, so it will have plenty of time to cook.

And if the dish finishes cooking before dinner-time, you can always switch the slow cooker to warm. If yours doesn't have a warm setting, you can always turn it off and then turn it back on about 30 minutes to an hour before you plan to eat.

Rebekah Meyer, Caldwell, ID

9. If you have made a hot drink ahead of time and are storing it in the fridge, make sure you give it 3 to 4 hours to warm up in the slow cooker.

Linda Spencer-Blackledge, Troutdale, OR

10. I have used my slow cooker several times at a potluck for hot, spiced apple cider or hot chocolate during the winter.

For early morning church choir rehearsals, I make hot Tang. It helps warm up our voices, plus gives a great-tasting dose of Vitamin C.

Linda Spencer-Blackledge, Troutdale, OR

11. We put the soft taco shells in the slow cooker to keep them hot and soft when we hosted a Tex-Mex supper for about 30 people. It worked very well.

Deloras A. Jordan, Riverview, FL

12. I de-boned a 21 lb. turkey before my guests arrived and kept it warm in broth in the slow cooker.

The carcass and the mess it creates was out of sight when guests arrived and the meat was so moist and tender.

Dolores S. Kratz, Souderton, PA

13. I bring my slow cooker to our Fellowship Meal for well over 100 people every Sunday. My slow cooker beans are always among the first to go. They are so simple and yet so appreciated.

All I do is this: before bed Saturday night, I place two pounds of dried beans and my special seasonings in the cooker, cover with water, turn on low, sleep well, and take to the Special Hungry Crowd.

Maryella Vause, Blanco, TX

14. We often do stone-soup meals using slow cookers for about 60 people at church. People are asked to bring something to add to the soup, so we don't know in advance what we'll get. It's important to use *everyone's* donation for a project like this.

Seasoning the soup correctly is the most important part of making this successful. I usually bring a bunch of minestrone-type herbs and extra garlic and onions to season the soups.

The biggest problem I've found with this sort of meal is trying to get the base ingredients started early enough to get the soup hot enough that adding a lot of more-sensitive veggies later won't cool it down too much and make us miss the 'time-to-eat' deadline. There's an amazing variation in cookers and it helps if you know the individual pots before starting.

Elaine S. Good, Tiskilwa, IL

15. Serving hotdogs for a large group? Use the slow cooker. It cooks them, keeps them warm and browns those around the edges. Adding less than ½ cup of water is plenty for a large slow cooker of hotdogs.

Shelia Heil, Lancaster, PA

Serving Crowds

1. Fill'em up, turn'em on and enjoy your party. It's so nice not having to constantly warm things back up or continuously fill serving bowls. You have time to attend your own party!

Ashley Watkinson, Chesapeake, VA

2. Use a fancier serving spoon to keep the food settings beautiful.

Jeanne Caia, Ontario, NY

3. Make sure your slow cookers are cleaned nicely because they will be sitting out and presentation is everything.

Molly Garza, Katy, TX

4. Make sure you use a "special events" slow cooker. My everyday slow cooker looks like it's been through a war!

Suzanne Steinbaecher, Lancaster, PA

5. I decorate my slow cooker for the event by decorating boxes that my slow cooker will fit in to match the party decor. I make a cord hole so I can keep it plugged in.

Ashley Watkinson, Chesapeake, VA

6. Place flowers and greens around the slow cooker to make it look attractive, or set the slow cooker in a basket of the same shape and have a fancy cloth under it.

Annie Boshart, Lebanon, PA

7. When I'm hosting a crowd at my house, I place my slow cookers strategically throughout the dining room, kitchen and family room to stimulate conversation and get people to mingle.

Molly Garza, Katy, TX

8. We used a slow cooker at a tea to keep the water hot for making tea.

Beverly Ronquillo, Marrero, LA

9. A slow cooker is a wonderful "punch bowl" for hot beverages. Just be sure to have the beverage hot and the slow cooker preheated.

Kelley Millemon, Alton, IL

10. I had cooked different kinds of soup and meatballs using my slow cookers for a big poker party. It worked out great. All the prep was done ahead of time, and the food was hot whenever we wanted to take a break.

Richard Dickson, Los Angeles, CA

11. I always thought using a slow cooker to keep homemade Chex mix warm for the party was pretty clever. As addictive as it is when it's cooled, I can't stop eating it if it's warm—and the aroma fills the house.

Richard Dickson, Los Angeles, CA

12. We used to avoid grilling hamburgers and pork patties on a Sunday after church if we were entertaining a large group. But we wanted to do a picnic-style meal, so my hubby grilled the meats for the sandwiches the day before, not overcooking them, and on Sunday morning, I put them in the slow cookers with a little water in the bottom, covered the top with foil before putting the lid on, and reheated them on low.

They were delicious. I am sure this summer we will be doing that a lot more.

Betty Detweiler, Centreville, MI

13. We bring chili, meatballs, or soups in our slow cookers to church functions and serve right from the slow cooker. It always goes very well. There's no preparation at church and the food is always very hot which is important and hard to do when serving a crowd.

Sharon Garber, Mahwah, NJ

14. During a party that lasts several hours, check the level of food in the slow cookers periodically, in case more liquid needs to be added, or the contents need to be stirred to prevent burning.

Cathy Fraser, Albuquerque, NM

Other Tips

1. What do you consider a big crowd? I cook for 10 kids everyday and use my slow cooker often!

Debbie Affleck, Elkins Park, PA

2. Ask to borrow extra slow cookers from friends or family if you don't have enough for a big event. Then you can send leftovers home in theirs without having to find containers that might not get returned.

Tress Hewitt, Torrance, CA

Cooking Away From the Kitchen

What To Take Along

1. Make sure you take potholders!
   Cindy Johnson, Galesburg, IL

2. Bring a *long* extension cord and masking tape to tape the cord down to the rug/floor.
   Mary Vaughan, East Amherst, NY

3. Make sure the slow cooker is close to the outlet. The cords are short on purpose because the manufacturers do not advise using extension cords.
   Nancy Kelley, Orlando, FL

4. If it's a carry-in event where there will likely be multiple cookers in use, I make sure there are enough outlets. If I'm not sure about the facilities, it's wise to have several outlet strips and a heavy-duty extension cord in the trunk, just in case.
   Kathy Thompson, Mount Vernon, OH

5. Put a note on top: "This is Barb's special pork roast — it is cooking!! Please do not lift lid! Does NOT need stirring!"

Otherwise, too many people lifting the lid lengthens the cooking time.

Barbara A. Elliott, Osawtomie, KS

6. Put a "don't peek" note on the lid because when the cooker leaves the kitchen, folks are more curious and easily tempted to tip the lid for a peek, thus delaying finish time.

Jan Mast, Lancaster, PA

7. Be prepared for everybody to ask you for the recipe and also ask you for a serving. Once people have been smelling it cook all day, they want some.

Melanie Luce, Carrollton, TX

8. If I am cooking something really aromatic and the family will be home all day, I cook in my garage. Otherwise, everyone is hungry all day long!

Deb Ward, Oxford, CT

9. I apply small sticky notes with the owner's name and dish contents to the lids and on the bottoms of the slow cookers. Everyone gets their own cooker and lid back at the end of the day.

Toni Thoma, Minneapolis, MN

10. Don't forget serving utensils. Don't get stuck trying to scoop out servings of scalloped potatoes with a red Solo cup!

Arlene Hall, Houston, PA

11. Mark your spoon if you want it back. Mark your slow cooker lid so you get the same one back that you took to the event.

Beth Bigler, Lancaster, PA

12. I prep as much as I can in advance. We like to have all of our ingredients prepared and in zippered bags so when we reach our camping destination, all we have to do is pour them into the slow cooker and we're done!

Jeanne Gibson, Ferguson, MO

13. Keep an extra utensil handy for extra helping hands or if a utensil drops outside. Also bring a storage container for any leftovers (which doesn't happen often) to either give away or transport back home.

Alys Corbin, Brick, NJ

14. The new slow cooker liner bags make clean up a snap, especially when I take my cooker to work and don't have an area to do big cleanups.

I just toss the liner after cooking and I don't have a messy cooker to carry home!

Coral Matich, Modesto, CA

15. Place a table against a wall to plug in the slow cooker so guests don't trip over the cords.

Dolores S. Kratz, Souderton, PA

16. I put the slow cooker on a sturdy table, close to an outlet. I tape the cord to the edge of table so if the table gets shook-up, instead of pulling the slow cooker off the table, it unplugs from the wall.

Andrea Rayna, Mt. Vernon, IA

17. When using your slow cooker away from the kitchen, make sure you put heat-safe protection under the cooker, such as a trivet or cutting board.

Tiffany Beka, Carlisle, PA

18. Take a piece of plywood or a cookie sheet to place under the slow cooker to level the pot and keep it from spilling.

Jean Moulton, Windsor, ME

19. Outside, keep the slow cooker in the shade. Cooking in a slow cooker in the sun doesn't work out so well because it tends to overheat and cook weird.

Kelley Bell, Cotopaxi, CO

In Vehicles

1. When I'm traveling and cooking using an outlet inverter for the plug in the car, I put the slow cooker in a milk crate to keep it steady.

I also cover the top with a towel so we won't smell the food as much. We get hungrier faster if we smell the good food cooking!

Ginger Dudek, Joliet, IL

2. When I use the slow cooker in our truck, I duct-tape the lid so it doesn't move too much when we're going down the road.

Malinda Irvine, Thompson Falls, MT

3. I had a friend who wanted to take healthy food with her on a road trip. She bought a power inverter for her car's cigarette lighter so she could plug in her slow cooker. She kept it on the floor during her trip, and when they stopped for lunch, she took the slow cooker out and served a healthy lunch to herself and her kids.

Deanna Wright, Leechburg, PA

4. We travel in a motor home 4 or 5 months of the year, and my slow cookers are my constant companion while on the road. I look forward to those times that we stop for over 48 hours in one place so that I can cook my slow cooker comfort food.

Norma Pratt, Brighton, Ontario

5. I took a lovely dinner to my widowed cousin in Watertown, NY. I started the dinner in the slow cooker at home in Canada in the morning. Then when my husband got off work, I unplugged the slow cooker, wrapped it in three layers of thick beach towels, and we took it in the motor home across the border. As soon as we got to Watertown, I plugged it in again and *voila!* dinner was all hot and ready to be served.

Norma Pratt, Brighton, Ontario

6. I put my slow cooker in the sink of our RV while we travel for a hot dinner at the end of our driving day.

Linda Spencer-Blackledge, Troutdale, OR

7. During the spring, we use the slow cooker a lot in our truck due to chasing 3 kids with 3 separate baseball schedules.

It is fun to watch people ask my kids where that plate of hot food came from when my kids walk up to the bleachers. When people find out I have dinner cooking or just staying warm in my truck while at baseball practice, they are amazed.

Malinda Irvine, Thompson Falls, MT

8. We have used the inverter in our vehicle to keep already prepared and wrapped chicken tortillas warm while we skiied.

Leticia A. Zehr, Martinsburg, NY

9. My husband and I used to drive a truck as a team and we had our little boy on the truck with us. Instead of eating out all the time, we used a slow cooker for at least one meal a day. We would sit the cooker on a ceramic tile on the floor and use it there.

I even gave my 10-year-old lessons on how to cook using our slow cooker on the road.

Lisa Raby, Mannford, OK

In Someone Else's House

1. I am a personal chef, and I use slow cookers to free up stovetop and oven space while making several different meals

through the course of the day for a client.

Jack Anders, Lindenwold, NJ

2. As a personal chef, I've gone into clients' homes and started meals in their slow cookers so when they returned home at the end of their day, dinner was ready and waiting for them.

Martha McKinnon, Phoenix, AZ

3. I sometimes fill my cooker halfway with ice cubes to keep a piece of meat frozen until I drive the 3-hour trip to my son's house where I can slow-cook dinner at his home.

This saves a hot, filled cooker from spilling over

on the floor of the back seat, and from taking a cooker and an ice chest.

Jean Robinson, Pemberton, NJ

4. Sometimes I need my slow cookers outside on the deck for my parties, or to take something delicious to someone else's place for their party, or to a cook-off-fundraiser for a good cause. My cookers have many miles on them.

Michael Feight, Eau Claire, WI

5. I cater a Thanksgiving meal for the fraternity my son was part of in college. The college boys love home cooking and don't care about the presentation of chafing pans which I normally use in my catering business.

This past year I used multiple slow cookers so I had less work with chafing pans and multiple roasters.

Of the four Thanksgiving meals I have catered for them, this last year using slow cookers was the easiest with the fastest cleanup I have ever had.

Also, transporting the food in the slow cookers

for the 45-minute journey was a great success because it all arrived still serving temperature!

Betty Detweiler, Centreville, MI

6. I have taken my slow cooker to a friend's house to fix dinner for all of us in the evening. Her husband works swing shift and my husband works days. My daughter is in her color guard.

My friend has small children and a very busy schedule, so instead of eating out or calling for pizza again, I brought a slow cooker and whipped up dinner and it was ready when we got off work.

Kelley Bell, Cotopaxi, CO

7. We are a military family, so we often stay in temporary housing when we move to a new base. I always bring at least one slow cooker with me, so I'll be able to prepare meals if we have to be out and about looking for a house or running some of the other errands involved with relocating. It also helps save money since we don't have to eat out for so many meals.

We have actually spent three Thanksgivings in temporary housing, so my slow cooker has helped to make a great holiday meal for my family to help us feel more at home during the transition!

Tress Hewitt, Torrance, CA

8. We have a clean up for my grandmother every year around her birthday and we used the slow cooker to keep hot dogs warm for the kids. This way we could enjoy the day without watching a pot.

Melissa LeClair, Frederick, MD

On Vacation

1. "Have slow cooker, will travel" is my motto. I have used my slow cooker on road trips when we have rented houses or cabins. I have used the slow cooker in our RV, and I have used the slow cooker at picnic sites when there is electricity.

I can spend more time with the entertaining and less with the cooking when I travel with my slow cooker!

Sonja Anderson, Folsom, CA

2. When using your slow cooker in a hotel, two things you should do are check to make sure you won't overload the circuit and put out your Do Not Disturb sign .

Sally Skupien, Spring, TX

3. We had a girls' weekend at a hotel and casino. To save a little money we had pulled pork sandwiches in our rooms, cooked in my slow cooker.

Jackie Crance, Grabill, IN

4. I used my slow cooker on a hotel room dresser when I traveled to Disneyland with my husband and six kids. We were in California for a week.

Before we got there, we planned out what we would cook each day, and made a grocery list of perishables we would need to buy when we arrived at our destination. We brought all other ingredients with us.

We ate every meal in our hotel room while we were there, with the help of our slow cooker. With eight people, we saved hundreds of dollars!

Machen Stephenson, Bothell, WA

5. I take my slow cooker to hotels for kids' hockey weekends. Even the kids get sick of fast food at sporting weekends, so we would plan — as a parent group — for sloppy joes, chili, pulled pork, etc.

Marilyn Groneng, Malone, WI

6. We took our slow cooker on our honeymoon.

Allyssa Stockton, Fountain, MN

7. We often rent a cabin or house for our vacations. I love to take my slow cooker along and start a meal in the morning before we go sightseeing. It's wonderful to come home to a home-cooked meal instead of waiting a long time in an overcrowded restaurant when we're all tired and grumpy. Plus, we save money.

Carna Reitz, Remington, VA

8. I reheat soup in my slow cooker when we camp.

Sara Dismore, Harrison, MI

9. I like using slow cookers at the camper. Not everything has to be grilled.

I made blackberry dumplings in mine at the camper and served them with fresh homemade vanilla ice cream. It was great!

Teresa Bennett, Newport, TN

10. When camping, the slow cooker is great!

I'll set it up before we go out hiking or tourist-ing and when we come back it's supper time. We are usually too exhausted to start a fire for cooking after a day of adventure and would rather just chat and roast marshmallows.

Colleen Van Dyke, New Holstein, WI

11. We use a slow cooker to make hot spiked apple cider at the campground on Halloween weekend. We decorate our sites, and the campground runs hay rides through the campground so you can see everyone's decorations. We make the hot toddies so we have a sip to keep us warm while we wait to scare the hay riders.

Cindy Carl, Barto, PA

12. I had a friend bring a slow cooker along tent camping once. She used the utility post the site had for campers and set the cooker on a cinderblock. It was excellent lasagna, and much appreciated since the boys didn't catch any fish!

Sherry B. Carrier, Levant, ME

13. I bring my slow cooker down to the boat dock with hot dogs, soup, dips or anything else we want. We get hungry after swimming and riding jet skis all day, and the slow cooker will keep hot dogs and brats hot and waiting for us.

Julie Bazata

14. I always take my slow cooker camping. Once you pay for your campsite, why use propane? Plus the slow cooker keeps the heat out of the camper.

It's also good for rainy days when I might not be able to cook over fire. I put it on the picnic table under the awning.

Beth Moss, Clio, MI

15. My slow cooker goes Up North every summer for family vacation. Put in the food in morning, fish all day, no dinner to prepare later.

I have even taken my slow cooker tent camping. I have set it up on the stump, plugged it into the electrical unit, and relaxed.

We are careful not to leave it out at night because of the bears.

Laurie Gunter, Woodbury, MN

Around the House

1. Out of sight sometimes means out of mind. I make sure to set a timer to remind myself to check the slow cooker periodically throughout the day.

Deb Ward, Oxford, CT

2. I use my slow cooker often on the dining room buffet where it is then its own serving dish. I have an outlet behind the buffet to keep it warm throughout the meal, so I guess it is also a warming plate.

Maryella Vause, Blanco, TX

3. The one thing I do not like about slow cooking is the odor of the food cooking that permeates the house all day long. I don't mind it if I am out for the day, but when I am inside all day, it's a bit much. I feel like I've already eaten whatever it is that I am cooking!

Barbara Nolan, Pleasant Valley, NY

4. When making sauerkraut, I keep the slow cooker out of the house to avoid lingering odors even though my family enjoys sauerkraut. I put the slow cooker on the patio in summer and in the garage in winter.

Dolores S. Kratz, Souderton, PA

5. I have used my slow cooker in my garage. I was cooking something overnight and didn't want the smell to bother my family while they slept.

Elaine Jones, Grand Rivers, KY

6. I used my slow cooker in a house being renovated. We put a board across the kitchen sink as there were no countertops.

Kathy Goehring, Wisconsin Rapids, WI

7. We were painting in the kitchen and had a mess all over the dining room and kitchen. I put my slow cooker on the back porch table so we could still have a nice meal.

Alanna Neupert, Cabot, PA

8. My home has a breezeway with a table and chairs in it. I take my slow cooker out there when the weather is warm and cook and eat there. It keeps my house cooler.

Martha Deaton, Fulton, MS

9. In the summer I put my slow cooker on the dryer or on the floor in the basement so my kitchen does not get so hot.

June S. Groff, Denver, PA

10. In the summer it's pretty warm in Florida, and even though we have air conditioning, we hate to heat up the kitchen. We put the slow cooker out on the patio table with an extension cord to an inside outlet, and everyone can get their food and not worry about the heat in the kitchen.

It's also nice when serving fish tacos or chowder that the smell stays outdoors.

Karen Mulhollem, Ocala, FL

11. Slow cookers are great in summer weather to keep all the cooking heat outside. We grill outside and have baked potatoes ready in the slow cooker.

Coral Matich, Modesto, CA

12. We use the slow cooker on the deck on the picnic table. Especially in the fall when the days are crisp and the sun is bright, hot food outside is a treat. We are trying to squeeze in the last days of eating outside before winter.

Barbara Gautcher, Harrisonburg, VA

13. During April 2011, the South was devastated by tornadoes. We were without power for weeks. Those of us who wanted to feed families that had lost everything plugged power strips into a generator, plugged the slow cookers into that and cooked so we had hot food to serve to people. Never expected that I would use my slow cooker like that!

Joy York, Wildwood, GA

14. Alton Brown of Good Eats has a slow cooker in his bedroom right beside his night stand. He puts oatmeal on to cook while he's asleep.

Garfield Rupe, Pulaski, VA

At Work and School

1. The slow cooker is perfect for work potlucks. It brings a variety of food that's easy to plug in once you get to work. Most work places don't have an oven, and microwaves just don't cut it for something big or something special.

Amy Schultz, Lancaster, PA

2. I've taken my slow cooker to work, but it made everyone hungry before it was ready!

Frances Raabe, Seattle, WA

3. I bought a slow cooker for work and always put something in on Thursday night for Friday lunch when the office staff would always eat together.

Joy York, Wildwood, GA

4. If you're using the slow cooker at work, get approval from appropriate supervisors first.

Kathy B. Jones, Frisco, TX

5. I was attending a morning meeting that I had traveled to the night before. All the attendees were to supply something for this breakfast meeting, so I decided that warm chunky apples would be delicious in the morning. I put them on when I arrived at the hotel that night and spent the night dreaming of cinnamon and woke to delicious apples that I was able to share with 14 others.

Kathryn Smith, Cuyahoga Falls, OH

6. I work in a beauty salon and not everyone gets to eat at the same time, so the slow cooker keeps soup hot and ready for whenever someone has a break.

Olga Rainey, Helendale, CA

7. We had an appreciation breakfast at work where we had scrambled eggs, waffles, bacon, and sausage links in lidded slow cookers to keep the food hot and moist since the employees ate in shifts. I didn't think about it at the time, but we could have had hot cereal also.

Kathy Thompson, Mount Vernon, OH

8. I've made chili in my slow cooker and sent it to work with my husband underground in a coal mine.

Candi Howman, Lewistown, MT

9. I have used my cooker at work — we have "Crock Pot Tuesdays." Every Tuesday at work, someone will bring a home-cooked meal in to share from their slow cooker. It's a great way to try others' foods and there's no need for takeout.

Shenno Luia, Corinth, NY

10. Probably the most unusual place I've used my slow cooker was in the classroom to make hot dogs and baked beans for my students to celebrate the last day of school.

Martha Deaton, Fulton, MS

11. I've taken my slow cooker to work at a feed mill.

Thomas L. Allen, Griggsville, IL

12. I take it to work once a week and fix my boss vegetarian dishes that I find online. She is a vegetarian and I have really enjoyed expanding my cooking.

Amy Fields, Bumpass, VA

13. I made a pot roast in the slow cooker and took it to work. It was especially appreciated because we worked overnight so there was no place open to eat and everyone was tired of eating cold sack suppers.

Cynthia McKean, Covington, WA

14. The oddest place I've seen someone else use their slow cooker is under their cubicle desk at work!

Amy Eckel, Harrisburg, PA

15. I have the lunch crock at my work and a 4-quart size also. I love having a healthier option instead of the fast food that the office gets daily.

Cindy Mishou, Kingsburg, CA

16. I used two slow cookers in my 5th grade classroom to make "stone soup" to go along with a lesson on working together and sharing.

Beverly Cowdery, Freeman, VA

17. I am a special education teacher, so I use slow cookers with my students because they are an easy, safe method of helping my students learn to independently cook healthy meals for themselves without the fears that sometimes come with using a burner or oven. We might have a one-dish meal or use three slow cookers for meat, potatoes, and dessert.

Everyone gets full to the brim and the rush rush of cooking is not there. There are easy leftovers to use, too.

Melanie Elliott, Poulsbo, WA

18. When my son was in high school, I used a slow cooker to keep hot dogs warm during baseball games. I would cook the hot dogs in the kitchen, put them in buns, wrap them in aluminum foil, and put them in the slow cooker. The slow cooker kept them warm at the concession stand.

I don't think this was my idea, I think this was just common practice since the baseball field was so far away from the concession stand at my son's high school.

Maura Flick, Orlando, FL

Other Odd Places

1. I don't think there's any odd place to use a slow cooker. As long as I have power, I'll do it.
   Michelle Clement, Elk Grove, CA

2. I attended a slow cooker cooking class where I and five other people brought our slow cookers. We prepared dishes in them, and then took them home to cook.
   Martha McKinnon, Phoenix, AZ

3. I've used my slow cooker on the frozen lake for an ice fishing party with co-workers.
   Edward Engelman, Menasha, WI

4. I've taken a slow cooker to church and plugged it in before the service when we've had a potluck meal.
   Esther Becker, Gordonville, PA

5. I usually take the partially-cooked food to quilt club and plug my slow cooker in at the meeting room on a card table with a very large hot mat under it. Set up is easy, and by noon it's ready so we can lunch on soup. My new recipes get tested by a group of ladies there.
   Jean Robinson, Pemberton, NJ

6. We use our slow cooker for apple cider at the sugar shack in the woods.
   Jackie McConnell, Napanee, Ontario

7. When we had a house fire and were living in a hotel for several months, I used my slow cooker nearly every day. The desk clerk and the maids said the smells coming from our room were fantastic and made them want to eat dinner with us.

Shelley Adams, Kane, IL

8. I used slow cookers in a stall in a horse barn so we could eat during an equestrian meet.

Roseann Howze, Howell, MI

9. We use slow cookers at our 4-H recycling center for hot cocoa and sloppy joes.

Renee Bisel, Evart, MI

Additional Tips

1. I make sure what I set the slow cooker on can handle the heat. I'm also careful to have a safe place to put the lid so it won't smash or leak condensation all over everything.

Christa Gettys, Rochester, NY

2. So that my lid won't get put on someone else's crock, I put one of my address labels on it and one on the outer electrical unit. When it's clean up time, I find my slow cooker easily.

Nancy Thackston, Gadsden, AL

3. I always place my slow cooker on a smooth, level heatproof surface. I've melted a few plastic tablecloths in the past!

I make sure to have a place to set the lid when serving, too: one of mine slid off the bannister on my friend's deck and shattered in the driveway below.

Arlene Hall, Houston, PA

4. Be cautious about what is set next to your slow cooker. I've have the knobs on my toaster melt as well as the cord when it touched the electrical unit.

Colleen Van Dyke, New Holstein, WI

5. Making sure that cords are not tangled and not up against the sides of the slow cooker is important.

Melanie Elliott, Poulsbo, WA

6. I have generally completed the cooking at home in my slow cooker, then used the warm setting when I get where I'm going.

Karen Schulz, Janesville, WI

7. As an Army family, we have moved often. I always take my slow cooker. That way while we are living in a hotel, house hunting or waiting to move in, I can make a hot meal without a stove.

Marianne White, Aberdeen, MD

8. When I arrive at my destination, I make sure to remember to plug in my slow cooker and turn the dial to the desired heat setting. My slow cooker can't work if I don't remember to turn it on!

Cathy Fraser, Albuquerque, NM

Stories About Special Occasions

Holidays

1. My family lives in the Southwest, and I use slow cookers for our annual Christmas Eve fiesta. Family members, friends, and neighbors gather at our house for a relaxing time during the hectic holiday season. Guests can help themselves to an array of Mexican dishes on a wintry evening.

My large slow cookers keep my green chile stew and posole warm on our festively-decorated buffet table.

I use my small slow cookers to keep sauces warm for guests to pour over my chicken ole' casserole. Beef and beans are ready to go in slow cookers for a build-your-own taco bar. Another slow cooker keeps my chile con queso dip warm for guests at our appetizer table.

We enjoy a relaxing evening filled with interesting conversations while we play board games, and make homemade ornaments.

Cathy Fraser, Albuquerque, NM

2. For Christmas 2009, we used an Italian theme instead of the traditional ham and scalloped potatoes. My sisters and I prepared sausages, sauce,

meatballs, lasagna, rigatoni, and chicken marsala in our slow cookers. It was a big hit with everyone.

Laurie Gunter, Woodbury, MN

3. I gave my friends a slow cooker for a wedding gift. One Christmas, the oven on their stove went out so they cooked the turkey in the slow cooker. They loved it and told me about it, so I tried it.

Now we like slow-cooked turkey because it doesn't dry out and it doesn't heat up the kitchen, which is warm enough here in central Florida at Christmas.

Nancy Kelley, Orlando, FL

4. I often make a seafood soup or chowder for Christmas Eve. Having it sit in the slow cooker for awhile gives the flavors a chance to blend together, and there's not much clean up when we leave for Christmas Eve services afterwards.

Norma Gehman, Ephrata, PA

5. We went to the Fredericksburg Winery in Texas and they were serving samples of a German Christmas wine, Gluhwein, in a slow cooker. I'd never known of a wine served warm before.

Becky Thompson, San Antonio, TX

6. I made barbecued pulled pork in my slow cooker for a Christmas party at work. The flavors and the tenderness were perfect. I started the cooking process the night before and then the next day took my slow cooker with me to work.

Everyone who walked past wanted to know what I made and what time we were eating. My slow cooker was empty before the fancy finger sandwiches were even half gone.

Melody Rauscher, Wantage, NJ

7. I think that the corn-bread dressing I made for Christmas 2011 was the best dish I've ever made in my slow cooker. I had to work half a day that day before dinner, so I had to put it in and pray that it would be okay, because there would be no time for a do-over. My mother-in-law had just finished chemotherapy and was in no condition to cook, so all of us girls cooked Christmas dinner and took it to the in-laws' house.

No one knew until I showed up that you could make Southern cornbread dressing in a slow cooker. It was so moist and delicious: my first attempt with that dish in the slow cooker, and it was the best I've ever made.

Having my mother-in-law still with us made that time very important to all of us.

Joy York, Wildwood, GA

8. I made corned beef and cabbage for our entire office on St. Patrick's Day, about 150 people. I used 17 crock pots and even had a vegetarian version.

Sonja Anderson, Folsom, CA

9. On Easter Sunday, we always have a sunrise service and then a potluck breakfast. This year, I brought my breakfast casserole in the slow cooker and

everybody loved it.

People just loved an option besides donuts and other sweets, but without the slow cooker, baked things usually end up cold.

Melanie Luce, Carrollton, TX

10. At one point our family's favorite recipe was Italian Chicken. My girls made if for me for Mother's Day one year. They worked so hard to make me a nice dinner and set the table very prettily. Italian Chicken is a white, creamy dish, and they served their favorite vegetable, beets, along side of it.

Well, when they were bringing the beets to the table my daughter slipped and dropped the dish and the pink liquid from the beets went flying.

We had "Pink Chicken" for dinner that night and laughed so hard because we kept finding pink beet juice in different locations all over the dining room during our dinner.

It was (and still is) my favorite Mother's Day dinner.

Melanie Luce, Carrollton, TX

11. At a holiday gathering, I decided to attempt a warm reuben dip which I never had tried before. I used fresh corned beef from the local butcher shop and fresh sauerkraut, too.

The dish was quite a hit and with the small rye bread slices, the dip was gone from the party in less than 35 minutes!

Kathryn Smith, Cuyahoga Falls, OH

12. My family gathered at my home owners' association clubhouse for New Year's and I hosted. There is no stove in the HOA clubhouse, just a microwave, so I brought one slow cooker of black-eyed peas and another of greens, plus a pan of corn-bread.

Nancy Kelley, Orlando, FL

13. The first picnic that I had with my new in-laws (100 of them) was on a very cold Memorial Day. I made my meatballs in my slow cooker and it was the only hot dish there. What a hit! Now they ask me to bring "the meatballs" for *every* occasion.

Gail Miller, Cambridge, NY

14. When my boyfriend and I had our first Thanksgiving together, we slow-cooked our turkey. Wow! It was delicious. Then we made a soup with the remaining turkey and stuffing, with veggies and broth. The stuffing was like dumplings in the soup.

It's now a tradition that we will make it the day after, and I like it better than the actual meal!

Shelby Sill, Dallas, TX

15. Our family loves stuffing and it is hard to get it out of the turkey and have enough for a full house of family.

Now I roast the turkey unstuffed and make the stuffing in the slow cooker so everyone gets enough.

Donna Clements, Hoquiam, WA

16. I made a sweet potato dish for Thanksgiving, for family members who did not think they liked sweet potatoes. It was successful because it was not overly sweet — no marshmallows involved!

Maggie Keyser, Iowa City, IA

17. My siblings and I remember our mom's wonderful dressing that none of us can recreate since measuring was not in her cooking vocabulary and she has passed on.

It always seemed the best, but now I think mine may be even better, and with so much less work.

Also, less stress at the holidays makes for a happy hostess. I use a recipe from one of the *Fix-It and Forget-It* books and have used it for about 5 years now.

Betty Detweiler, Centreville, MI

18. We served Thanksgiving dinner for 25 in our basement after our house was flooded this past October 2011. It was a thank-you dinner for all who helped to clean up and scrub the walls to make it livable again.

Annie Boshart, Lebanon, PA

19. My son was away at Thanksgiving and missed his favorite traditional Thanksgiving meal. Not wanting to cook a large turkey and go to the effort involved in our usual holiday meal, I cooked the stuffing and a turkey breast in the slow cooker when he came home. We all agreed it was the *best* turkey and stuffing we've ever had!

The slow cooker made it possible for me to treat my son to a traditional family meal without the usual effort required. The meal was truly delicious, he loved it, and it made me feel wonderful to be able indulge the family without breaking my budget.

Meg Trager, Ellicott City, MD

20. My Thanksgiving Day dressing is the favorite of several generations. It has two secrets. First, I make the broth in the slow cooker long before Thanksgiving. Second, I saute the veggies in butter and add them to the pot with lots of homemade broth before the cornbread crumbles. It makes a moist and flavorful side to the turkey.

Maryella Vause, Blanco, TX

Parties

1. I slow cooked all the food for my wedding reception for about 50 people. My mom and I went to the store the day before the wedding, then got up in the morning, prepared and got all the food cooking. Everything turned out amazing.

Deanna Wright, Leechburg, PA

2. A friend was getting married and doing her wedding on a frugal budget. Her oven broke, however, so I brought all of my slow cookers and we just put Italian Wedding soup, BBQ and a Chocolate Lava dessert in the slow cookers to cook.

Molly Garza, Katy, TX

91

3. For mine and my cousin's wedding receptions, we had a total of 12 slow cookers going. Both receptions were great successes and everyone raved about the food.

They also liked the fact that we had built a family tradition into the wedding. In our family, we bring slow cookers to most of our holiday celebrations, so it was fun to have that as a part of our weddings.

Allyssa Stockton, Fountain, MN

4. When my son, a Marine, came home from his first tour in Afghanistan, we had a huge welcome-home, potluck dinner for him. All he had requested was meat. He had gone 6 months on chicken and was hungry for *meat*! So many family and friends arrived with every kind of meat, cooking in slow cookers in every way you can imagine. The love and support from everyone for my son, welcoming him home, was very touching and an event we will forever remember.

Katie Francis, Wanette, OK

5. I took a slow cooker into work once for a surprise party for our boss. We had the metal sign company next door keep the cooker in their garage, so that our boss wouldn't see it or smell it.

Josie-Lynn Belmont, Woodbine, GA

6. I hosted a get-together for about 40 people. It was themed "Beans & Greens" and I cooked 4 different types of beans: pintos, navy, black-eyed peas, and limas. I also cooked 8 full-size bags of turnip and mustard greens, cornbread and all the trimmings.

I used the slow cookers to keep everything hot after it was finished cooking. I could not have pulled it off without my slow cookers!

Everyone had a great time, and I didn't have to worry about anything burning or boiling over.

Joy York, Wildwood, GA

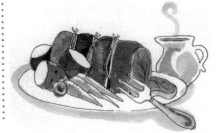

7. There were almost 200 people at our house for my husband's 45th birthday party. Every slow cooker in the county was at my house with food in it! Everything stayed hot, and no one had to run back and forth tending to food, so everyone was able to enjoy the party.

Joy York, Wildwood, GA

8. I borrowed slow cookers from my mom and nephew to use for a special birthday dinner for my son. His birthday fell on a weeknight, and I knew I wouldn't have time to cook a special dinner once we arrived home from a day of school, work and his golf practice. So I planned a slow cooker meal that I knew he would love.

In crock #1 we had Beef Enchilada Casserole, crock #2 was creamy potato soup and crock #3 was a hot fudge lava cake. I served the meal with a green salad and a veggie tray.

He loved his birthday meal, and we all loved that it was ready when we got home!

Marsha Neeley, Cookville, TX

9. Every year I host a dinner party for my brother's birthday. He did so much remodeling work for us that I honor him in this way. I invite his closest friends, so it usually ends up being 10-12 people.

I have done many theme dinners, but last time we did a murder mystery dinner. I did a jerk pork roast in my slow cooker that came out just delicious! And by the way, he was the murderer!

Mary Vaughan, East Amherst, NY

10. I made slow cooker macaroni and cheese for my daughter's birthday party. It was great for all the kids. I unplugged the cooker and just kept the lid on until serving time, to allow the macaroni and cheese to cool to a "just right" temperature.

Maureen McCarthy, Framingham, MA

11. My daughter's birthday party had six slow cookers going. I had macaroni and cheese, Spanish rice, lasagna, mashed potatoes, apple spice cake, and peach cobbler. This

way there was something for all the picky eaters.

Cindy Mishou, Kingsburg, CA

12. We have a monthly birthday breakfast at my office of about 30 men... and me. My occupational field of IT is dominated by men, so I'm the only woman in my office. They don't cook, but instead give me money.

I know men like meat, so for the breakfast, I always buy a pre-cooked beef bris-ket from our local grocery. I let it cook all night and in the morning I shred it with forks. I serve with warm

tortillas, shredded cheddar and BBQ sauce. The guys love it and look forward to the event each month.

Becky Thompson, San Antonio, TX

13. I was out on a run (I drove a semi-truck at the time), and my son's birthday party was going to be the day we came in, so I made a quick call to my brother and sister-in-law and they fixed the birthday dinner. Two slow cookers had wet kitchen towels in them to heat up store-bought tamales; the other cooker had chili cheese dip.

When we got home, there was a full house of teenage boys enjoying themselves. I almost didn't get any tamales!

Lisa Raby, Mannford, OK

14. When my first grand-daughter was born, I wanted all of our friends and family to see her. The problem was I did not want to burden my daughter, the new mother, with having a party. I decided to throw a "Baby's First Day at Grand-ma's" party. I invited about 35 close friends and family

over to see her.

Out came my two slow cookers, and I borrowed another three. We had Italian sausage ravioli with spinach and white bean soup (slow cooker #1), roast beef (slow cooker #2), rice pilaf (slow cooker #3), meatballs (slow cooker #4), a cheesy potato dish (slow cooker #5), green salad, relish tray, rolls, green beans, rice pudding, and cake.

Everyone certainly had enough to eat, and it was so nice that I could sit and visit with everyone, because the slow cookers did almost all of the work.

Mary Vaughan, East Amherst, NY

15. I am known for baking, decorating, and selling desserts from my home. Every occasion we're invited to, I make at least one dessert.

Once I made a cake in the slow cooker. It was funny to see everyone looking around and asking why I didn't bring a dessert, but when they started smelling the cake, they knew!

Of course, I was proud to take the empty slow cooker home.

Delilah Swinford, Anderson, IN

16. I surprised my in-laws with a 50th Anniversary picnic. I made all of the food for 45 people. The menu included turkey barbecue, pulled pork, hamburger barbecue and baked beans, all of which I cooked in my slow cookers. Come picnic day, I used the slow cookers to keep the food hot.

Susan Bickta, Kutztown, PA

17. When my late husband retired from the military, one of the dishes I made for his party was sweet and sour moose balls. People raved, even after I told them that the meat used was moose.

Judy Sondergaard, Boulder City, NV

18. My favorite event was when we had a fondue party theme and everyone brought a different something to "dip". We set up 4 slow cookers with a different sauce in each.

It was special because it was fun and different and no one expected it to be a "tidy" experience, yet it was sort of elegant.

Colleen Van Dyke, New Holstein, WI

19. We always have 2 soup suppers at the campground where we are seasonal campers: one when we open to see each other after the long winter months and one before we close for the season to bid goodbye to our fellow campers.

We all make our favorite soup to share and bring them to the recreation hall in slow cookers which keeps them warm enough until we all eat. We have placards for each soup and line them up on the tables. We pull numbers to see which table gets to go first. People get to try 3 soups the first round.

After everyone has had one pass through, the buffet is open for anyone to go back and get more. It's so much fun! If you really like a soup, you find out who made it and get the recipe.

There have been anywhere from 25 to 50 slow cookers full of soup.

Cindy Carl, Barto, PA

20. I have a soup party every year as a great way to break up winter up here in upstate New York. People bring their soup in their slow cookers; we've had as many as 14 different soups. It's an unusual party when you have to cook in order to come to it, but people actually ask if they can come!

Bonnie Sorensen, Laurens, NY

21. I cook many dishes in my slow cooker that receive rave reviews, but I would have to say the one that generates the best reaction from everyone is a White Chicken Chili recipe.

The first time I made it was for a movie night at my house with some gals from work. They never stopped talking about it and went back for seconds and even thirds. They all left with the recipe in hand!

I think it is a perfect combination of

"just enough spice," cream cheese making it thicker and richer, and the shredded chicken a nice change from traditional ground beef chili.

Rebecca Key, Boulder City, NV

22. A family reunion that I hosted in my home for 13 people was easier because the slow cooker helped in making large quantities of tasty food. My guests were thoroughly impressed and asked for all the recipes.

I also made breakfast in the slow cooker and then my guests were amazed! They all vowed to go home and get their slow cookers out.

Rebecca Key, Boulder City, NV

Other Special Occasions

1. Every time I use the slow cooker it seems like a special event. The food always turns out so good!

Melissa Kinnaird, Gallipolis Ferry, WV

2. All family gatherings and celebrations are special occasions in our home. Over the years I have used my slow cookers for birthday parties, graduations and holidays. What makes life so special to me is my husband and our six children. As our family is expanding with our children's spouses, I'm going to need my slow cookers more than ever!

Sheryl Gudgeon, Chambersburg, PA

3. I made my vegetarian chilli for a cook-off and won first place. Five pounds of exotic mushrooms in two slow cookers, and the men judges thought it had meat.

Amy Freeman Marquez, Brevard, NC

4. I made a white bean chicken chili in my slow cooker and entered it into a chili cook-off. I won first place! It was the first time I had ever won anything.

Ambriel Mccathern, Austin, TX

5. I made wassail in the slow cooker for a Madrigal Dinner put on by my daughters' high school choir. The flavor was authentic and the aroma really added to the ambiance.

Susan Johnson, Minneapolis, MN

6. I took a version of the hashbrown casserole with cream soup, butter and gobs of cheese in my slow cooker to a meeting day at work.

Since I was new there, I didn't know that everyone just picked up something at the store deli or bakery to contribute to the turkey our boss was bringing.

I was the only one who brought something home-made, and the divine aroma nearly killed us all before we finally got to eat.

Sandy Olson, Turton, SD

7. My mother is now 86 years old and is no longer able to cook. Growing up, I always thought she made the best home-made vegetable soup in the world. She lives 4 hours away from me, and when I go to visit her, I love taking a slow cooker full of the same homemade vegetable soup that she used to make for us growing up.

Addie Calvitt, Durham, NC

8. I was doing a last-minute fundraiser for a family whose father died

and they needed money to help cover burial costs. We didn't have enough roasters, so I called my friends and asked them for their slow cookers. We made more than enough money to cover the bills.

Ginger Dudek, Joliet, IL

9. My good friend and neighbor's dad was in the hospital and she was spending a lot of time there. I have a key to her house to take care of their dogs and cats when they aren't home. I fixed up a pot roast with potatoes and carrots and took it over to her house one afternoon so that the meal was all ready when she and her husband got home from the hospital.

She said their dog met them and the door and took them straight to the kitchen to show them where the wonderful smells had been coming from. I can't imagine the anguish I put that dog through, having to smell the cooking meat all afternoon.

Nonetheless, my friends were thrilled to have dinner ready when they got home!

Carna Reitz, Remington, VA

10. I loaned my 3-pot buffet server slow cooker to a friend whose son had died, and I also provided three different homemade soups.

The family had relatives arriving at different times from around the country to stay at and near the family's home. With bread and salad accompaniments, the soup meal was little fuss or muss for the family and a nice presentation for the out-of-town relatives.

Judy Faro, Dallas, GA

11. I cooked moose stew for the Iditarod in Alaska. After the initial start in downtown Anchorage, mushers proceed to Eagle River at the VFW. The mushers eat moose stew and then pack up their dogs and go to Wasilla, where the race officially starts. It is a tradition to cook the moose stew and the mushers love it.

Judy Sondergaard, Boulder City, NV

12. When we went to a ball game, someone hit a foul ball which landed on top of the slow cooker.

The lid broke and spilled the apple pie, but we managed to save a little pie to eat!

Arlene J. Wells, Orland, IN

13. I once made an amazing lasagna in my slow cooker for neighbors. It was to help them through a death of a loved one. They loved it as just the right comfort food.

Growing up Italian, I was shocked to make a successful lasagna in a slow cooker!

Robyn Buck, Willow Street, PA

14. When we adopted my son, I made some soup in my slow cooker for his homecoming because I knew I would be busy with him.

Amy Fields, Bumpass, VA

15. My friend had just had surgery, and I didn't know what type of gift to get her to welcome her home from the hospital. I decided that if it were me, I'd want someone to cook my dinners. So I got out all 4 of my slow cookers and made and froze her enough meals for about two weeks.

I now do this for a lot of my gifts for friends, including Christmas gifts.

Emajoe Abeln, Cordova, TN

16. We have an annual chili cook-off at our church in October. It's held in the upper part of a barn and people vote for their favorite chili with donations to the church building fund. The one with the most money wins. Of course, there's a lot of friendly stuffing of the boxes to make your husband's chili the winner, plus add more to the building fund!

Barbara Gautcher, Harrisonburg, VA

17. I made shredded barbecue pork for a potluck at church. It was awesome because people thought it was a lot of work, but all I did was season the pork, cook it overnight, and it was done in the morning. No work at all!

Aileen Melendez, Chicago, IL

18. We attended a newly-formed mission church that held worship services in a rented building, rather than in a traditional church.

Once a month, we would gather together after the church service for an afternoon of fellowship over a potluck lunch. Since we didn't have a kitchen at our disposal, most families brought slow cookers to keep food warm during the worship services.

Several international families attended the church, and brought interesting dishes from their homelands to share with everyone. The food sure smelled heavenly as it cooked during the services!

One time there were so many slow cookers lined up in a row on the rectangular tables for a Thanksgiving potluck, that my preschool son said, "Look, Mommy! It's a food train!"

Cathy Fraser, Albuquerque, NM

19. At the school where I taught a kindergarten reading program, the staff wanted to do something fun for the students on "Go Western Day." With permission from parents and the principal, each of the teachers brought a slow cooker and chili ingredients to school. The ingredients were assembled, none of them too spicy, and the slow cooker started first thing in the morning while the students observed the first stage of the chili cook-off.

All day, the aroma filled the classrooms. Later that afternoon, each student got a spoon and the teachers took turn dishing up delicious chili into tiny cups for each student to sample a variety of chilis.

It was a wonderful way to add a little flavor to a day of learning, and the students absolutely loved the grand finale to a special day.

Yen Parrott, Houston, TX

Cooking
Tricky
Foods

Pasta

1. I don't cook pasta in the slow cooker. I cook it on the stovetop and then add it to the slow cooker during the last 20-30 minutes of cooking time. Otherwise, I end up with a starchy blob in the bottom of my pot.

Angel Barnes, Kinderhook, IL

2. I tried making a double batch of macaroni and cheese to keep warm in the slow cooker for an all-day occasion. Believe me, you do *not* want to keep cooked pasta in the slow cooker all day, even set at low.

What was left was either browned and hardened around the edges or totally broken down.

Susan Bickta, Kutztown, PA

3. I cook pasta separately and add it to the slow cooker near the end.

Esther Becker, Gordonville, PA

4. I usually use the slow cooker to reheat or keep a pasta dish warm. It's a good way to take it to a picnic or fellowship meal.

Crystal Trost, Harrisonburg, VA

5. Whole wheat pasta cooks slower, so I usually use it in the slow cooker.

Colleen Larson, Plain City, Ut

6. I keep cooked pasta separate and add it to individual servings at the table.

Suzanne Steinbaecher, Lancaster, PA

Boneless Skinless Chicken Breasts

1. Know your slow cooker! The perfect amount of cooking time for boneless skinless chicken breasts on high in my slow cooker is 3½ hours, but recipes often call for 4-6 hours on high for chicken breasts.

Sheryl Rogener, Tracy, CA

2. I never cook boneless skinless chicken breasts in the slow cooker by themselves. I add other veggies, etc.

Janet Peterson, Pierz, MN

3. I place chicken breasts on top of vegetables.

Kathleen Felmey, Gresham, OR

4. Chicken breasts in the slow cooker always come out nice for me, but I put them on a bed of celery first.

Linda Nelson, Ormond Beach, FL

5. I shorten the time the boneless skinless chicken breasts are in the slow cooker.

Michelle Clement, Elk Grove, CA

6. I put either a few pieces of romaine lettuce or cabbage leaves on top of the chicken breast. These can be discarded after cooking.

A half cup of chicken broth is also helpful to steam the chicken.

Jean Robinson, Pemberton, NJ

7. I marinate boneless skinless chicken breasts in yogurt the night before cooking. There is some kind of enzyme in the yogurt that makes it more tender. I have also used half-and-half to marinate them, too.

Rebecca Dumas

8. I wrap chicken breasts in prosciutto or bacon and lay them on a small grilling rack.

Molly Garza, Katy, TX

9. I keep boneless skinless chicken breasts whole when cooking, then I shred or chunk them in the last half hour of cook time.

Tiffany Beka, Carlisle, PA

10. Boneless skinless chicken breasts must be cooked in liquid or they will dry out. I keep an eye on the clock and remove them when they are done. Otherwise, even if I turn off the cooker, they will continue to cook in the hot liquid.

Nancy Kelley, Orlando, FL

11. I make sure to put enough liquid in the slow cooker. I use cheap white wine.

Linda E. Wilcox, Blythewood, SC

12. I use lots of marinade for boneless skinless chicken breasts. Also, fresh whole mushrooms on top are a great source of moisture for any meat.

Michael Feight, Eau Claire, WI

13. I prefer boneless skinless thighs—they get done much faster than most people realize. And I don't add too much liquid unless I actually want stewed chicken!

Barbara A. Elliott, Osawtomie, KS

We include tips from various viewpoints so you can make your own fully-informed decision. For example, some cooks have different methods for cooking chicken breasts. Think of this book as a circle of cooks, discussing their experiences and preferences. We hope you benefit from all of that as you decide how to proceed.

14. I only cook boneless skinless chicken breasts until they reach 165° and then I take them out of the slow cooker.

Cindy Carl, Barto, PA

15. I prefer to use boneless, skinless chicken thighs in the slow cooker, but if I have breasts I just cook them for less time.

Jill Brock, Rochester, NY

16. I make sure I have a good sauce for boneless skinless chicken breasts. I find cooking slow and low is most successful.

Alys Corbin, Brick, NJ

17. I put boneless skinless chicken breasts in the middle layers of the dish, so there's something on top of and also underneath them.

Amy Fields, Bumpass, VA

18. I cook boneless skinless chicken breasts half as long as recipes say, and use my meat thermometer.

Ellen Stier, Oceano, CA

19. I make sure to use something that nearly covers the chicken breasts—soup, salsa, gravy, broth, anything that would give them flavor and moisture.

Sheila J. Moline, Reno, NV

20. The one thing that I learned early on when cooking meat in the slow cooker was not to use too much liquid for roasts and chicken. I add only enough to come about half way up meat. It is delicious.

I used to cover roasts with broth, and they always came out tough.

Terry Bartlett, Orlando, FL

21. Don't add too much water. When I roast a chicken, I season it well and put it in a slow cooker with no water. It comes out delicious.

Candi Howman, Lewistown, MT

22. I never cook a meat without bones in the slow cooker.

Anna Free, Fairbanks, AK

23. I don't have very good luck with boneless skinless chicken, so I use bone-in pieces with the skin still on.

Olga Rainey, Helendale, CA

Milk Products

1. I add milk during the last 30 minutes of cooking only.

Addie Calvitt, Durham, NC

2. I do not add milk until right before serving, and I turn off the slow cooker right after adding it.

Maura Flick, Orlando, FL

3. As in stroganoff, I add milk or cream at the very end, *not* while the dish is boiling.

Karen Mulhollem, Ocala, FL

4. I add warm milk as close to the end of cooking time as possible.

Jeanne Gibson, Ferguson, MO

5. I don't usually use dairy milk or cream in the slow cooker. I use almond milk, soy milk, or coconut milk from time to time. If I do use dairy milk or cream, I usually add it toward the end of the cooking time.

Melanie Luce, Carrollton, TX

6. I use evaporated milk or heavy cream only.

Gayle Hall, Harbor, OR

7. I substitute an equal amount of evaporated milk for the regular milk in a recipe. Or if the recipe calls for a small amount of cream, I use an equal amount of plain Greek yogurt or sour cream, stirring it in during the last hour of cooking.

Arlene Hall, Houston, PA

8. Using a cooked roux is a good method to avoid curdling.

Also, I don't add dairy with acidic ingredients. If possible, I substitute at least in part with condensed soups or add the milk during the last hour of cooking.

Dorthy Erlandson, Pullman, MI

9. If I thicken the milk by making a white sauce with it, that prevents curdling.

Carol Eveleth, Wellman, IA

10. I temper the milk or cream with the hot liquid from the slow cooker. Then I pour the milk and liquid mixture back into the slow cooker.

Lori Stewart, Mulberry, FL

11. I heat the milk first in the microwave in a bowl, then I add it to the slow cooker.

Shawna Rowan, Saint Marys, GA

12. I heat the milk in the microwave before I put it in the hot slow cooker. I sometimes have trouble with sour cream, so I heat that first also.

Barbara Yoder, Christiana, PA

13. I don't use milk or cream in slow cooker recipes. Cheeses are usually fine.

Arianne Hochstetler, Goshen, IN

Altering and Converting Recipes

From Stovetop to Slow Cooker

1. One hour of simmering on the stovetop or baking at 350° F in the oven is equivalent to 8-10 hours on low or 4-5 hours on high in the slow cooker.

   Deanna Wright, Leechburg, PA

2. A guideline I found online at one time has been very helpful.

   Oven or stovetop: 15 to 30 minutes = 1½ to 2½ hours on high, or 4 to 6 hours on low.

   Oven or stovetop: 35 to 45 minutes = 2 to 3 hours on high, or 6 to 8 hours on low.

   Oven or stovetop: 50 minutes to 3 hours = 4 to 5 hours on high, or 8 to 18 hours on low.

   Ann Thompson, Maryville, TN

3. My basic rule of thumb is that for 1 hour in the oven at 350°, figure on 4 hours on high or 8 hours on low in the slow cooker.

   Carna Reitz, Remington, VA

4. Try new recipes, and use old recipes as a guide.

Neva Mathes, Pella, IA

5. If I try to convert a recipe to the slow cooker and it works, I write it on a recipe card and save it for future use.

Tess Vowels, Belle, MO

6. Figuring out how to make regular recipes in the slow cooker is my new hobby!

Kris Riddervold, Ballston Spa, NY

7. For soups and chili, I just usually throw everything in the slow cooker for about 4 hours on low if it calls for an hour to simmer on top of the stove.

Amy Schultz, Lancaster, PA

8. Veggies need heat *and* liquid, so I put them on the bottom or along the sides of the cooker to be sure they get done.

Arlene Hall, Houston, PA

9. If I'm converting a rice dish, I use long-grain rice, not instant.

Nancy Robb, Cadillac, MI

10. I think the most unusual recipe I have used my slow cooker for was for making Chex mix. Chex mix is traditionally made in the oven, but I decided to make it in the slow cooker one day. It did require frequent stirring, but it turned out great. The flavors of the seasonings had fully mixed into the cereal and the whole batch was nice and warm when it was done.

Noel Bigelow, Bellefontaine, OH

11. When I was a child, my mother used to make homemade spaghetti sauce from scratch. She would let it simmer on the stovetop for hours to blend all the flavors.

I have taken my mother's homemade spaghetti sauce recipe and adapted it for the slow cooker, so I can have one of my favorite childhood meals as an adult without spending all day in the kitchen.

Noel Bigelow, Bellefontaine, OH

12. One day I wanted to make applesauce for my children, but I didn't want to be tied to the kitchen and the stove all day. Put on my thinking cap, and *voila!* Apples in

the slow cooker on low for 6 hours, then use the potato masher.

Melanie Miller, Flemington, NJ

13. The recipes I have converted did not require much modification. For soups, I make sure to add raw vegetables early in the cooking process to get the most flavor and best tenderizing.

Addie Calvitt, Durham, NC

14. My mother-in-law would make home-made Italian spaghetti and meatballs from scratch and let it cook the entire day on the stove; needless to say, she would occasionally burn it.

When I received my first slow cooker, I took it with me to visit the in-laws and had her put the sauce in it to cook all day. The sauce maintained its rich, robust Italian flavor and was a big hit.

Molly Garza, Katy, TX

15. My husband loves Thai dishes. So I took his favorite Thai coconut

chicken soup dish and made it in the slow cooker. I had to tweak it a bit, but it came out so good that my husband asked me over a dozen times that night, "Are you sure you wrote down this recipe?"

I think slowly adding the spices and then tasting was the key to getting this recipe just right. Too much spice as well as too little can ruin a dish

Frances Raabe, Seattle, WA

16. I grew up eating Lebanese food because my aunt is Lebanese. We found mjadra, a traditional Lebanese dish, to be even better in the slow cooker than on the stovetop.

Hope Comerford, Clinton Township, MI

17. We just have a lot of fun with soups and make all kinds. They're based on what we have on hand and we experiment with herbs and spices. The end result is always a surprise and we've never had a bad soup, some absolutely awesome, but hard to remake!

Andrea Rosenfield, Jacksonville, IL

18. I've made omelets in my slow cooker. I put hot water in and turn it on high. Then I place 2 eggs in a plastic food bag along with a tablespoon of butter, cheese, onion, ham, mushrooms, shrimp, anything I want in the omelet. Mix. I seal the bag and put in the slow cooker. I let it sit in there until the eggs are set up or until I'm ready to eat.

Michelle Clement, Elk Grove, CA

19. Our absolute favorite is my black peppercorn French dip sandwiches. They're spicy and flavorful, tender and juicy. They were kind of an experiment that worked out wonderfully. I used to purchase this marinade for bbq'ing and one day just decided to try it on a roast in the slow cooker. It came out so well we kept doing it.

Michelle Clement, Elk Grove, CA

20. Our favorite slow-cooker food is yogurt. I make it with one quart of heavy cream and one quart of whole milk, plus the yogurt starter. It comes out thick like a Greek yogurt.

The exciting part that we've just been experimenting with using this creamy yogurt to make ice cream! We don't have an ice cream maker, so I just add sugar, vanilla, and other flavorings and pop it in the freezer. It's our favorite treat!

Eve Mercer, Hebron, ND

21. I have started cooking whole chicken or chicken legs with no added liquid. I dust the meat with dry spices. It is just like roasting—they actually get browned.

If too much liquid builds up, I spoon it off because whatever chicken is below the broth will not get browned. I add barbecue sauce at the end and slightly vent the lid so that it will candy instead of liquify.

Sometimes I do the legs in the slow cooker and then put them on the grill for the last few minutes to smoke them up.

Beth Moss, Clio, MI

22. I like to do ribs in the slow cooker. I cut them into portions of 2 bones each, layer them with onion slices between, and add in water and barbecue sauce. They come out so tender they practically fall off the bones. I remove the meat and thicken the sauce to spread on the ribs.

This is so much easier than boiling and baking, and the taste is fabulous.

Janene Walker, Macomb, MI

23. My favorite way to make baked sweet potatoes is to put them in the slow cooker with a bit of water and basically steam them. The sweet potatoes are so soft and delicious. They are never dry like they tend to be in a microwave or oven. Lovely!

Norma Grieser, Sebring, FL

24. I used my slow cooker once to heat water for coffee when my coffee maker broke. I wrapped the coffee grounds in cheese cloth and it worked in a pinch to serve coffee.

Randi Kubit, Strongsville, OH

25. When I'm converting a regular recipe to the slow cooker, I cut the salt in half. I always use sea salt, then I add a bit more near the end to brighten the flavor. I think iodized salt in the slow cooker lends a metallic flavor (but I'm weird).

Andrea Rayna, Mt. Vernon, IA

26. I started making my fruit butters in the slow cooker. They do not overcook and the consistency comes out great. I then use a hand-held immersion blender to blend it the cooked fruit into butter.

Kathaleen Jones, Rancho Cordova, CA

27. I make jams, fruit butters and sometimes chutneys in it, depending on the recipe. I hate standing by the stove, so this way is much easier, much faster, and the results taste great. I cherish my slow cooker —I can't imagine life without it!

Kathaleen Jones, Rancho Cordova, CA

28. Homemade apple butter works great in the slow cooker. Yum! I don't have to watch the apples as much as when I made it on the stove. I will leave the lid off for a bit to thicken the "sauce" into "butter."

Ronda Hall, Great Falls, MT

29. The only things I don't like in the slow cooker are crisp vegetables like broccoli and cauliflower. They can get too mushy.

Jeanne Gibson, Ferguson, MO

30. If you want the finished dish crispy, like fried chicken, do not cook it in the slow cooker.

June S. Groff, Denver, PA

31. Experiment, and then invite boys over. They will eat anything.

Laurie Gunter, Woodbury, MN

32. I used recipes for years but recently have started making up my own creations. After you get more experience with how your slow cookers work, you can start being really adventurous!

Sarah Herr, Goshen, IN

Handling Liquids

1. Be careful using liquids because the food has its own natural fluids. Unlike other cooking methods, the slow cooker retains all the moisture.

Kathy Hildebrand, Rochester, NY

2. Usually if a traditional recipe calls for a cup of liquid, I may use ¾ cup when I make it in the slow cooker. The steam creates moisture in the dish.

Beverly Cowdery, Freeman, VA

3. Don't put too much liquid in — I have seen too many dishes ruined because people forget the liquids already in the food. Start with small amounts because it's easier to add than to remove.

Barbara A. Elliott, Osawtomie, KS

4. The most important thing I've learned is

about how much liquid is produced with slow cooking. I've learned to decrease liquids if I'm trying to convert a regular recipe to the slow cooker.

Meg Trager, Ellicott City, MD

5. I frequently modify soup recipes for the slow cooker. Because of the high liquid content it's fairly foolproof.

Tina Schwab, South Attleboro, MA

6. Once your prep is done and in the slow cooker, you need to make sure there is room for liquids. If you fill the cooker too full,

you will have seepage from under the lid and over the edges.

If you weren't trying to make soup but you add too much liquid, you will have soup.

Melody Rauscher, Wantage, NJ

7. I have found no need to add water to any recipe or any meat that I cook in the slow cooker. They produce their own juices to cook and marinate in, and the water only dilutes that.

Rebecca Key, Boulder City, NV

High Versus Low

1. I sometimes start out my food in the slow cooker on high to get it bubbling, and then turn it to low because I don't like the idea of raw meat sitting on low.

Jeanne Caia, Ontario, NY

2. A jump start on high for an hour is a good way to boost the melding process. I set a timer to remind myself to turn it down!

Deb Ward, Oxford, CT

3. I stir the dish if it starts to brown around the edges.

Debbie Caraballo, Manahawkin, NJ

4. When I cook on high in half the time, the dish sometimes gets a little brown around the upper edges, but often tastes quite good.

Tiffany Beka, Carlisle, PA

5. If it is the first time or two that you have altered a recipe to cook on high instead of low, I would suggest that you be home when you try this, just to make sure the recipe doesn't dry out and burn.

Michelle Parks, Newark, OH

6. I prefer to cook my food on low for a longer time, but I have cooked stew on high for half the time. It was okay, but I think low and slow is the way to go.

Julie Bazata

7. I prefer to cook low and slow. If I don't have enough time for that, I usually won't use the slow cooker.

Carol Mathay, Shoreline, WA

Doubling Recipes

1. Does the recipe call for an ingredient that will be larger when cooked than it is before cooking? Dried beans, rice, dehydrated meats and vegetables—all of these things get bigger

while cooking because they absorb a lot of water. If there is something in your recipe that has this trait, I recommend not trying to double it until after you've tried it as a single recipe first. If, as a single recipe, it fills your cooker half way or less, then it should be safe to double.

Angel Barnes, Kinderhook, IL

2. When preparing baked goods or cheesecake in the slow cooker, it's best to prepare several batches as opposed to trying to double the recipe.

Molly Garza, Katy, TX

3. I double almost anything except baked goods. I do not exceed ¾ of the height of the crock.

Tiffany Beka, Carlisle, PA

4. Make sure that the slow cooker won't be more than ⅔ of the way full of ingredients, so that the ingredients will cook evenly.

Cathy Fraser, Albuquerque, NM

5. I make sure I have the time to extend the cook time when I'm making big recipes. It's always better to have too much time than not enough.

Colleen Van Dyke, New Holstein, WI

6. A doubled recipe will take longer to cook, although not double the time.

Shelia Heil, Lancaster, PA

7. The amount of spices and seasoning doesn't always need to be doubled when making more, so I add extra seasoning lightly. I can always add more if needed, but I can't get it out.

Vicki Pittman, Elm City, NC

8. A larger recipe may need to be stirred during the cooking process. This avoids cold spots in the center of the dish.

Shelia Heil, Lancaster, PA

Small Recipes

1. Use the right size slow cooker. That's why I have different sizes. The more spread out the ingredients are in the crock, the more chance they will dry out or burn.

   Tina Schwab, South Attleboro, MA

2. To make a small portion of food, I make sure to use a smaller slow cooker so that it is at least ½ full, but ideally ⅔ full.

   Karen Bussema, Crete, IL

3. I use a smaller slow cooker. I don't try to do small portions in the 5-quart size slow cooker.

   Marla Beihl, Garden Grove, CA

4. Use the right size slow cooker! My husband once made nacho cheese dip in the largest size cooker I have. It was a burnt solid mess for about 2 inches, with only about ½ cup of edible cheese! Pretty funny now.

   Deborah Schule, Corpus Christi, TX

5. To make a small portion of food in a large slow cooker, I put the food in a smaller dish inside the crock.

   Julie Hamilton, Lititz, PA

6. I use a water bath with a smaller pan set in the center of the crock to make smaller recipes in a large cooker.

   Jeanne Gibson, Ferguson, MO

7. Now that the kids are grown up and on their own, I realized that I wasn't eating healthful meals anymore because I really didn't know how to cook for just one person.

   Then I figured out that I could make bigger batches of food in my slow cooker and freeze it up in one-person sized portions. At dinnertime, all I need to do is pop something in the microwave and I have a nutritious homemade meal. No more dollar menu for me!

   Gaille Robertson, Wheat Ridge, CO

Cooking with Kids

Picking Recipes

1. Perhaps the biggest job of slow cooking with children is helping them to plan ahead. On weekends

and during the summer, the child can fix the recipe in the morning or early afternoon for that evening's dinner. During the school year, the child will probably need to prepare the recipe the evening before the day of serving it.

Phyllis Pellman Good, Lancaster, PA

2. I tell my kids, "If you can read and follow directions, you can cook." I do help them pick recipes that are easy to follow.

Nancy Thackston, Gadsden, AL

3. I use the slow cooker the most at my house, but my 10-year-old son has gotten more involved with cooking. He asked for the *Fix-It and Forget-It Kids Cookbook* and now enjoys using the slow cooker to make dinner for us all.

Tina Schwab, South Attleboro, MA

4. A slow cooker recipe is good for kids to start learning to cook. They don't have to stir food while it cooks in a hot pan on a hot stove.

Martha Deaton, Fulton, MS

5. I got the *Fix-It and Forget-It Kids Cook-book* and a 4-quart slow cooker for my daughter for Christmas when she was 8 years old. We both love the recipes in it.

Tasty Tomato Soup was the first one we tried. It was so easy, she did it all herself. There is just something about the flavor that we can't get enough of. Even my sister, who doesn't care for tomato soup, asked for the recipe.

My daughter and I make this often. It's something she likes to put together on winter mornings before school, and when we both get home, we know a good supper is waiting for us.

Also, since it's just the two of us, we always have leftovers, and I freeze them in one- and two-serving size containers.

Linda Knippen, Delphos, OH

6. I let the kids pick out a recipe on their own, no matter how new it is to me. I find out things they like that I never knew about.

Shenno Luia, Corinth, NY

7. I found a *Fix-It and Forget-It Cookbook* several years ago, and we tried several recipes out of it. On the covers and the front page, we have written some of our own recipes and throughout the book, we have written our own changes to the recipes in the margins.

When it started getting close to time for my son to move out on his own, the only things he requested were a copy of that book and a cooker for himself!

Lisa Raby, Mannford, OK

8. My son loves to sit with me to look through our cookbooks to find recipes to make for the week. I let him choose the recipes he wants to make. That gets him excited about the cooking process and ensures he will stay interested and keep at it until he has finished the recipe.

Then we make the grocery list together. It teaches him that planning and cooking are a process, and that the food doesn't just magically appear on the table each night—someone has to work hard to make it!

Brisja Riggins, Dorado, Puerto Rico

9. Always have Plan B for the meal in case the creative recipe doesn't work out.

Terry Bartlett, Orlando, FL

Tasting and Peeking

1. I tell my children not to open the lid to peek every five minutes as it slows the cooking process.

Stephanie Ringler, Weston, OH

2. I let them taste, and then I ask their opinion about what the dish needs.

Gina Greene, Springfield, VA

3. I remind them that what they are making is for the whole family so they can't lick the spoon or their fingers until everything is in the pot and cooking.

The rule is: "When the top goes on, the licking goes on."

Beverly Cowdery, Freeman, VA

Measuring and Mixing

1. I have them measure ingredients into separate bowls before adding to them to the slow cooker. Otherwise, they could spill an ingredient directly into the slow cooker and ruin the recipe.

Cathy Fraser, Albuquerque, NM

2. Put the pot on a level low enough that the kids can see inside as they add food to it.

Beth Bigler, Lancaster, PA

3. Mix the ingredients in an unbreakable bowl, not in the slow cooker crock. It can break if it falls.

Cindy Mishou, Kingsburg, CA

Safety Concerns

1. I always make sure the slow cooker hasn't been turned on yet so it doesn't get hot for them to touch.

Cindy Johnson, Galesburg, IL

2. Slow cookers are hot: the food inside and the outside surface. Keep the appliance sitting far enough back on the counter when cooking.

Molly Garza, Katy, TX

5. Don't let the cord hang down over the edge of the counter where little curious hands can pull it down and spill the hot contents on themselves.

June S. Groff, Denver, PA

6. I find that slow cooking is a safe way to introduce cooking in the early learning center when I work. The smells are wonderful and the children can see the change in the ingredients as they cook.

Judy Slenker, York, PA

3. I pre-cut ingredients for knife safety, but I let the kids layer and season.

I also allow them the freedom to add "special" ingredients that aren't in the recipe.

Patty Paulsen, South Jordan, UT

4. I usually do most of the preparations that require cutting, but the kids like to measure and put ingredients in the crock.

Beth Bigler, Lancaster, PA

Methods and Thoughts on Teaching Kids

1. One mom who wanted her 12-year-old twin sons to have some meaningful activities during the summer, handed the boys a *Fix-It and Forget-It Cookbook*. She asked each of them to choose one recipe per week that they'd like to make.

They made the grocery list for their individual recipes, and the mom did the shopping. Together they decided who was cooking on which day.

The boys were old enough to handle the food preparation. They needed to use the stove very little to make the slow-cooker dishes, so the mom had fewer safety concerns.

The guys happily ate the food they fixed, they gained some cooking skills and greater acquaintance with food, and the mom had some serious kitchen relief!

Phyllis Pellman Good, Lancaster, PA

2. I have had to buy a slow cooker for each of my daughters as they move out on their own to make sure they didn't sneak mine into one of their boxes.

Susan Johnson, Minneapolis, MN

3. I let the kids do everything. I stand back and just stay there if they ask for help. It builds confidence, and they are so proud to eat something they made.

Tina Schwab, South Attleboro, MA

4. Be very patient. Remember, children have a shorter attention span than adults. They want to please you so much and to help.

Praise them for a job well done. If you have to correct them, do so kindly and be sure you aren't a perfectionist. It is all about learning and family time.

Stella Fagan, Jacksonville, AL

5. My young-adult daughter was moving out and a month or so after she moved, I was looking for my slow cooker. I found out she took it to make her own porketta, her favorite slow cooker recipe that we used to make together.

I had to buy a new slow cooker!

Kathy, Hibbing, MN

6. It is so much nicer to be able to work together on a meal when we aren't all hungry and tired! Everyone is fresh and ready to work because we aren't cooking just before mealtime, so the experience is much more enjoyable for everybody. Plus, the kids can add all the ingredients to the slow cooker before they turn it on, so no worries about anyone getting burned.

Tress Hewitt, Torrance, CA

7. I am a second-generation slow cooker queen. My late mother did a lot of cooking in a slow cooker, and my daughter has fallen right in line behind me. And we plan on the three granddaughters doing the same.

I just wish I could let Mom know about all the neat new recipes there are now!

Karen Phillips, Mantei, NC

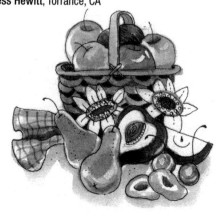

Stories of Everyday Slow Cooking

Favorite Meals

1. My siblings and I live in different states, and my mother always prepared vegetable soup on the stovetop for us when we came home for a visit. Now, years later, we have all adapted that to the slow cooker and have it waiting when we visit each other.

   Virginia Rose Hartman, Akron, PA

2. I have a trio buffet set and I left dinner for my husband. I had a meatloaf in one, vegetables in the second, and dessert in the third. He loved it!

   Theresa Carrell, Lewisville, TX

3. I am a teacher and work long hours after school. The slow cooker

enables me to make healthy meals instead of getting takeout.

Patricia Slattery, Hopewell Junction, NY

4. I make many meals in my slow cookers and take them over to my hard-working girlfriend who doesn't have (take) time to cook. It keeps me in good graces with her.

Michael Feight, Eau Claire, WI

5. I think the story behind the our favorite slow cooker food goes back a number of years when our second son was about 6. He would tell his other siblings not to eat all the roast beef and au jus gravy as mom was going to make veggie soup in the slow cooker from the leftovers the next day. Veggie soup was his favorite food as a kid and still is today.

Linda E. Wilcox, Blythewood, SC

6. I had a washer repair-man who had to make several visits to our house, comment on how good my house always smelled at supper time. My youngest son said the food always tastes that good, too, and invited the man to dinner.

Julie Bazata

7. I made shredded pork, snap peas, broccoli and soba noodles in a ginger peanut sauce on a whim for myself. It was *so* good. The pork was so tender after cooking all day, then I added all other the ingredients and they melded together.

Jen Farrington, Shelburne, VT

8. I purchased a *Fix-It and Forget-It Cookbook* years ago and was amazed by all the food items that could be made in the cooker. I always thought it was for beans and soup only. I decided to try several dishes.

I love lasagna, but hate the mess so when I tried it in my cooker, it was love at first bite! It is such a different meal for the slow cooker to most of my friends that they always ask for the recipe. I am now able to have lasagna more often without all the mess.

Sheila Diggs, Lubbock, TX

9. Now that my husband and I are empty-nesters, I enjoy cooking a turkey breast in my slow cooker for a wholesome meal without all the fuss of a big bird in the roaster.

Jan Moody, Olive Branch, MS

10. I was making chicken tacos for my family, since we were running in every direction that day, which is really the story of our life. I threw the ingredients into the slow cooker, and literally forgot about it.

When we got home after a long day, the aroma of the chicken filled our home, and the smiles on my family's faces were priceless!

Celia Thompson, Hartsville, SC

11. Slow cooker mac and cheese is my wife and daughter's favorite dish. Then we always get creative with the leftovers and make grilled mac and cheese sandwiches—kids love them.

Jeramy Lawrence, Aurora, CO

12. I was cooking Sunday dinner for my husband. I posted what we were having on Facebook and got several phone calls requesting the recipe.

I made my own version of Monterey chicken by changing up a recipe with some poblano peppers, bacon, two types of mushrooms, and two types of cream soups. I also added two types of cheese at the end. It was served with cilantro lime rice. It was so good!

Ambriel Mccathern, Austin, TX

13. I especially love using the slow cooker for Sunday lunches. I can get it going and go to church without worrying about having to come home and cook as it will be ready when I get home.

Janet Peterson, Pierz, MN

Special Memories

1. I work part time and my sons were very involved in sports. We were at a ball park sometimes 7 days a week.

The slow cooker was an easy way to make sure we all had home cooked food, even if we ate in shifts.

I was a stickler for home cooked meals. I would even bring my kids a hot meal up to the ball park to eat on a break.

We saved lots of money and calories in all those years; otherwise, we would have had nachos, pizza, hotdogs and popcorn for meals—no way!

Beth Moss, Clio, MI

2. In winter, my late husband and I might get home 3-4 hours after leaving work. At that time, there was one road to Eagle River from Ft. Richardson. If the weather was bad or there was an accident, we sat in traffic long enough to read a short book, or knit a scarf.

How wonderful to walk in the door and dinner was ready in the slow cooker! Pork chops with mushroom soup, beef stew, etc.

Judy Sondergaard, Boulder City, NV

3. When we were first married, we did not have any pots or pans. We had a slow cooker and an old fryer, both from a yard sale. Since we had no stove, we kept them on the radiator in the bedroom.

We lived off soup, stew, chili and mounds of French fries.

Elf Noyes, Columbia, MO

4. I use the slow cooker the most at our house, but about 10 years ago, I had some serious medical problems that temporarily kept me out of the kitchen. My husband would bring in the ingredients I would need, and would set up a tray for me, and I would prepare everything, and he would "tend it" for me. He even learned to make a couple of things, himself.

Josie-Lynn Belmont, Woodbine, GA

5. One very rainy, cold and windy day, I decided to make a beef stew in my slow cooker.

About halfway through the day and about halfway through things cooking in the slow cooker, we lost electricity. We called the power company for status and found out it could be a good 24 hours before power would be restored.

So, out came the candles.....and then it dawned on me. What about my beef stew in the slow cooker? My husband, being a handyman and quick thinker, quickly found our little Honda generator and plugged my slow cooker in and fortunately was able to finish cooking a wonderful beef stew on such a stormy night!

Dana Hagy, Loomis, CA

6. My daughter, fiance and I love to pick apples fresh from the orchard. When we have made as many things as we can out of the apples, we take what is left and make slow cooker apple butter.

Dorthy Erlandson, Pullman, MI

7. The only problem I ever had in slow cooking was that my cat liked to knock the lid off the slow cooker and eat the food. We locked him in the bathroom to solve the problem.

Beverley Williams, San Antonio, TX

8. I use the slow cooker most in my house, but others do make use of it too. My husband and my oldest son like to cook breakfast on the weekends. Sometimes when I have an early morning class, I get a wonderful surprise when I get home!

Sherry B. Carrier, Levant, ME

9. I began cooking supper once a week for three households when kitchens underwent renovations. I only had a slow cooker to

12. At one point I tried most of the recipes in a *Fix-It and Forget-It Cookbook* that I purchased from a local grocery store. I have stars next to the ones that were hits with the family.

Since then I tend to make up my own combinations. I work 9-5 every weekday, so I use the slow cooker almost every day to prepare dinner.

Maura Flick, Orlando, FL

use for two years. Nobody minded except me, and only then when I had to wash everything in bathroom pedestal sink. Amazing what you can adapt to!

Melissa Hoyt, Havelock, IA

10. I had to call a committee meeting at a somewhat inconvenient time, so I made dinner for the attendees with my slow cooker.

John Bradford, Saint Charles, IL

11. I used the slow cooker in my garage once when my son hosted his fraternity's executive meeting. They had to have a private meeting and it was raining outside, so they used the garage and I set the slow cooker up with chili inside for them.

Paula Byers, Marietta, OH

13. We are from PA and went to a cabin in the mountains of VA. For dinner, a roast beef was put in the oven on low for 3 hours.

Friends of ours from PA were visiting mutual friends living in VA. We decided to surprise all of them with a visit using a map we at the local service station. We thought the 2 hour trip would bring us back in time to enjoy our roast beef dinner.

After driving up and down, around the many curves of the mountains for 2 hours, we still had not reached our destination. And the roast was in the oven back at our cabin! The map did not show us the numerous turns and steep mountains. Being able to drive only 20-35 miles per hour lengthened our trip time wise.

We could only visit with our friends a few minutes because we needed to get back to our roast which was still in the oven, back at the cabin, which was a 3-hour return trip.

When we returned with dread to the roast, we found it amazingly done to perfection. Now we use a slow cooker with this roast recipe to eliminate the stress of possibly burning the roast.

June S. Groff, Denver, PA

14. When we were selling our home, I would try to establish a "homey" atmosphere with baked desserts, breads, or a slow cooker meal cooking on the counter. The smell was inviting for those who came through at a showing.

Betty Detweiler, Centreville, MI

15. Back in 1975 when we lived in Kansas, my husband was working 90 miles away from home.

On Friday, I would get the slow cooker going early, then make rice and a salad. When school was out, I had the car all packed, and the slow cooker wrapped in towels and secured on the floorboard of the car. Our three kids would change their school clothes, and we would drive out to where my husband was working.

We would be at the motel when he got in and after a shower, we would all sit down to a good meal.

Joy Goade Zowie, Beeville, TX

16. My sister's oven went out and she borrowed 3 slow cookers until she could purchase a new stove. She cooked for a family of 6 for 2 months.

Barbara Gautcher, Harrisonburg, VA

17. I made a slow cooker lasagna for my family and they loved it! We were outside working in the yard all day and they didn't know I had prepared it. They were so surprised when dinner time came and it was all ready and super-delicious.

Suzanne Steinbaecher, Lancaster, PA

18. My six kids always loved a big pot of queso while they were doing homework. I can't even imagine how many homework assignments were turned in with little blobs of cheese here and there. This was a particular favorite in the winter when the snow was blowing, and it only took second place to banana bread fresh from the oven.

Gaille Robertson, Wheat Ridge, CO

19. I had my dad and brother over to eat with my husband and me. It was the first time I had guests over to eat at our apartment since we got married. I worked that day, so the slow cooker took the pressure off to get home quick and make something. It was great.

Leanne Skoloda, New Holland, PA

Signature Recipes

1. This year is the first time I made candy in my slow cooker. It was peanut clusters and they were so easy and delicious that I've made them a couple more times!

Cindy Johnson, Galesburg, IL

2. My family loves meat loaf, but I forgot to put it in the slow cooker one morning and had to resort to putting it in the oven. My family never let me forget how much they didn't like it from the oven, so I only used the slow cooker from then on.

Eleanore Fiori, Marquette, MI

3. I make a zesty vegetable beef soup that always disappears quickly. Using spicy V8 and Worcestershire sauce gives it an extra zing, but those flavors just don't work unless they've been slow cooked. I tried it on the stovetop once and it was not even close to the same thing.

Susan Johnson, Minneapolis, MN

4. The thing I make the best in my slow cooker is my clam chowder. I make it every year when we have a fish fry. Maybe it tastes so good because we are eating it outside in the fresh Maine air, or maybe because I made it!

Lisa Henry, Sanbornton, NH

5. I was a high school cook for 33 years, and it was hard for me not to just make everything on a stove or oven at first, but once I used a slow cooker, I was hooked. We love to have chili made in the slow cooker. The flavor is fabulous.

Janet Peterson, Pierz, MN

6. My mom likes to fix a side like macaroni and cheese in a slow cooker for family reunions. She has arthritis, so doing something like that is much easier on her, plus she can spend more time with family.

Amanda Payne, Pilot Mountain, NC

7. My most successful dish is Brunswick Stew. It takes me 3 or 4 days to make it. I slow cook roast beef one day, pork roast another day, and chicken another day.

When all the roasting is complete, one pound each of these meats is mixed together with the rest of my recipe.

The flavors are delicious! My family begs me to make it more often. The good news is that it makes a large recipe, so I can freeze many meals.

Deb Ward, Oxford, CT

8. Our favorite slow cooker recipe is rump roast. I always rub the meat with salt and then brown the meat in the oven for 45 minutes before starting the slow cooker. I add the meat and ½ cup water and then cook on low about 9 hours.

My dad was over for dinner one night. He asked what kind of meat it was since it was so good. He did not believe me when I told him. He said his wife's roasts were never that good.

Jolene Wallace, San Antonio, TX

9. The week after my husband and I were married in 1974, we attended a reception for his older brother and new wife. My mother-in-law served these killer meatballs. I asked for the recipe and she gave it to me.

Later, she submitted the recipe as her contribution to a church cookbook they were publishing.

Now, I have become well known for these meatballs, but I always give my mother-in-law credit as it was originally her recipe. Even my husband's coworkers ask for these meatballs, so my husband hauls the slow cooker in to work.

Recently, I made the meatballs for Thanksgiving dinner appetizers with my husband's family, and my mother-in-law asked me for the recipe! I told her it wasn't mine, but hers, but that thanks to her, I was well known for my excellent meatballs. She didn't believe me or remember them from the wedding reception 30-some years prior. I didn't convince her until I pulled the church cookbook off her kitchen shelf and showed her her own submission!

Sandy Olson, Turton, SD

10. I make our favorite dish, pot roast, for my family frequently. It is delicious, comforting and everything is in one pot for easy clean up. I love to quilt and sew, so this kind of meal gives me lots of extra time for my quilting.

Donna Clements, Hoquiam, WA

11. I used my slow cooker to smoke a brisket. It turned out wonderful. I don't cook on the grill myself, so instead of having to wait for the hubby, I did it in the slow cooker. Wow, it was great!

Linda Ince, Amarillo, TX

12. I am known by my family to always have something in my slow cooker. During the cold winter months, I am always making some kind of soup or stew. If someone isn't feeling well, I'll get a request to make my hearty chicken or lentil soup. It's always a hit.

Melody Rauscher, Wantage, NJ

13. One of my successful slow cooker dishes is wild turkey legs and noodles. It is successful because wild turkey is so tough, but the slow cooker makes it wonderful!

Tonya Dias, Baker City, OR

14. When I made carnitas in the slow cooker, the spices had time to infuse into the meat which just melted apart.

That night we had the best tacos of our lives.

Katherine Heldstab, Pittsburgh, PA

15. I make a great vegetable beef soup which uses taco seasoning to season the beef. All the vegetables are fresh, and I leave the green beans whole. I add a handful of pasta at the last minute. I also like to saute the vegetables in butter prior to adding them to the pot.

I always get raves about this soup, and I've served it for dinner guests, parties and potlucks.

My secret ingredient is love. I always hold my guests in my mind and heart as I prepare the soup, and I think it adds a special flavor to the soup.

Richard Dickson, Los Angeles, CA

16. I think in general everyone likes my shredded beef best. It makes the house smell good and is wonderful to come home to.

When a Mexican restaurant came to town and started offering shredded beef burritos, I thought "I can do that" so I did.

Alexis Roy, Sauk Rapids, MN

17. My pulled pork is my best slow cooker dish because my kids and husband take it for lunch the next day and it tastes even better.

Donna Porter, Schaumburg, IL

18. My daughter and husband are fans of barbecue, especially chicken.

At my daughter's insistence, I tried a recipe for cola chicken that used ketchup and cola to make a barbecue-type sauce for the chicken. My daughter can't get enough of it!

In fact, I have to triple the sauce when I make it because she likes it with the chicken poured over noodles. I have even given this recipe to her group home to serve.

Kathryn Smith, Cuyahoga Falls, OH

19. Homemade tomato sauce tastes best when cooked all day in the slow cooker. This is the most delicious food I make in it, and there is no mess on my stove!

Phyllis Kirchdoerffer, Fair Lawn, NJ

20. My dad *loves* my beef stew, which is a recipe I got from a *Fix-It and Forget-It Cookbook*. He says it tastes just like the stew he had in the Hungarian army! That doesn't sound like a compliment, but if you knew my dad and his sense of humor, it is.

Jill Bishop, Wallingford, CT

21. I have made stroganoff, often with venison, for many people for when they have babies or are sick. They all seem to love it and want to recipe.

My niece was a first time mother and didn't cook. She wanted to learn, so I made it for her at her house in her slow cooker and gave her some other recipes. She actually started cooking.

Beth Moss, Clio, MI

22. Just this past year I made pumpkin butter for the first time. I had heard of making apple butter in a slow cooker, and wondered if I could do it with pumpkins. We had been given six of them and I didn't want to waste the food. So I researched and found it was possible!

I used spices I had on hand and by the end of the day, my family had pumpkin butter that tasted like pumpkin pie! They prefer it over apple butter.

Sheryl Gudgeon, Chambersburg, PA

23. My family and co-workers would all have to agree my best recipe is a tie between my chili recipe or my beans. They ask for them both

a lot! What could be better than a warm comfort food cooking and filling up the house with cooking scents?

I think those two recipes benefit the most from the slow cooking as it really brings out the flavor.

Deborah Schule, Corpus Christi, TX

24. The best dish I've made in the slow cooker is a flounder Veracruz. I made it just for us and it was so delicious.

I think it was successful because slow cooking the sauce really allowed the flavors and spices to marry well.

I froze the sauce right after it was cooked and then on a week night, defrosted it and cooked the fish in it. We had a very classy meal with no work.

Natalia Armoza, Gardiner, NY

25. I had football playing boys and by far, their favorite recipe was "Mom's Carnitas Burritos." The boys would invite all of their friends over and create their own enchiladas. They all agreed mine were better than Chipotle restaurants.

Laurie Gunter, Woodbury, MN

26. I love comfort food and am drawn to the recipes that I ate as a kid, as is my husband. I love surprising him with dishes that remind him of his childhood.

One of the best is my Mom's simple recipe for stew meat and gravy. Everyone loves it.

Martha McKinnon, Phoenix, AZ

27. Being a deer hunter's wife, I was always trying to find ways to cook the meat in a way that everyone could enjoy it. Cooking it in the slow cooker makes it so tender.

I love to put a nice piece of deer round steak in the cooker with plenty of sliced onions, sliced green peppers, and garlic. Then I add a package of dry onion soup mix and let it cook all day — it turns out so yummy and tender. I make stews, soups, roasts and BBQ deer for sandwiches.

In fact, my slow cooker is the only way I cook deer — except for cooking the tenderloins on the grill.

Susan Ervin, New Philadelphia, OH

28. When my son isn't feeling well, he asks for chicken cooked with carrots, potatoes and onions. He always asks me to mash the vegetables and add a little broth from the crock with a spoonful of sour cream.

He says this comfort dish makes him feel like his mama loves him when he is sick.

Brisja Riggins, Dorado, Puerto Rico

29. My best recipe is my pulled pork. Being from Kansas City, we are known for BBQ. But it takes so long to cook.

I throw it in my slow cooker overnight with liquid smoke and root beer. It cooks on low throughout the day and then there's a yummy dinner.

Barb Long, Kansas City, KS

30. My mac and cheese has always been a hit. I am able to season it the way our family likes it.

Plus, I serve it with bowls of add-ons like bacon, broccoli, and mixed veggies so we can create our own crazy concoctions.

Cindy Mishou, Kingsburg, CA

31. Our twin girls were runners in high school. I would slow cook 2 lbs. of stew meat, 2 cans of mushroom soup, and 2 onions cut fine, and serve it over egg noodles. They called it "Runners Delight."

Suzanne McCandless, Scott City, KS

32. My chicken enchilada slow cooker casserole is always a success because the ingredients blend well and make a creamy, rich, not too spicy dish that everyone seems to love.

If I'm having guests, I'll make a double batch and serve it with a crispy green salad and some tortilla chips or homemade rolls to mop up the sauce. It saves people from the embarrassment of trying to lick their plates!

Gaille Robertson, Wheat Ridge, CO

Non-Food Slow Cooking

Crafts

1. I use my old slow cookers with shallow cracks or too much crazing on the crock to be used for food for dyeing silk and nylon fabrics/scarves and scrubbies with acid dyes.

   The lids, crocks, and electrical units are clearly marked with permanent markers so they don't migrate back to the kitchen.

   Elaine S. Good, Tiskilwa, IL

2. I use my slow cooker to heat tea or coffee for staining fabric for crafting. It's easy to soak the fabrics.

   Donna Davis, Horse Cave, KY

3. I have used my slow cooker to dye fibers for my crochet projects.

   Katie Francis, Wanette, OK

4. I have used a small slow cooker for melting wax for batik. It was never used again for food, only crafts.

   Katrina Pawlaczyk, Jackson, MI

5. I make sure to line the crock with a liner bag or tinfoil when I'm using it for things like wax.

   Janet Peterson, Pierz, MN

6. The campground we stay at has tie dye activities but the dye water needs to be warm so that the dye holds color. Being outside cools the water of quickly, so the campground uses old slow cookers on warm to keep the dye water warm.

Sonja Anderson, Folsom, CA

7. I have used aluminum cupcake liners to melt broken crayons into mixed colored disks. It takes a couple hours to melt down, and then I stir them a little to mix them up. I let the whole thing cool, and then peel the liner off the colors.

Vickie Cook

8. Melt candle wax inside of another can using the slow cooker to act as a double-boiler.

Michelle Parks, Newark, OH

9. My husband used one of my slow cookers to keep water at a hot, steady temperature. He placed a container in the water bath to melt wax to make hand-dipped candles.

Sheryl Gudgeon, Chambersburg, PA

10. I use the slow cooker to make soap and to dye my wool yarn. It keeps the ingredients at just the right temperature without losing the temperature, unlike a stove.

Trina Mechling, Warren, OH

11. I had an expensive, scented candle that was misshapen but still had loads of wax, so I put it in a quart jar and set that inside my small, dip-size cooker. Worked like a charm!

Julie Hamilton, Lititz, PA

12. I use a small slow cooker for keeping hot glue melted while doing long drawn-out projects like wedding items. It saves tons of time not having to continuously pick up the glue gun.

Beverly Cowdery, Freeman, VA

13. I am an art teacher. I retired my old slow cooker without a removable crock and filled it with water for softening craft plastics. It works great!

Kathy Thompson, Mount Vernon, OH

14. I make refrigerator magnets out of modeling clay. I set them on a small rack in the bottom of my slow cooker with the lid off to dry them overnight. They are ready to paint the next day.

Toni Thoma, Minneapolis, MN

15. We used the slow cooker to melt candle wax and to make homemade soap. It's a slow steady heat so things don't scorch.

I read about a woman who used hers to make homemade laundry soap, but I am not that industrious.

Andrea Rayna, Mt. Vernon, IA

Beauty

1. If you are going to use your slow cooker to melt paraffin wax for manicures or pedicures in or to make candles, buy one dedicated for that use only.

While the wax is easy to remove from the insert after it cools, no one wants to eat food from something you dipped your feet in to coat them in paraffin. It doesn't matter that your feet were clean and that the crock has been washed clean, no one wants to eat where your feet have been!

Joy York, Wildwood, GA

2. My daughter uses hers to melt wax for waxing her legs.

Janet Peterson, Pierz, MN

3. My hair lady keeps her eyebrow wax in a slow cooker.

Linda Knippen, Delphos, OH

4. I saw a slow cooker used for a makeup show. It was keeping an oatmeal mask warm.

Rachel Scott, Sioux Falls, SD

5. A friend who sells Mary Kay uses a small slow cooker to keep water warm for wetting wash cloths for people to wipe makeup off their faces.

Donna Davis, Horse Cave, KY

6. You can also use some herbs to give yourself a facial steam. I use rose water and put the slow cooker on high. I cover my head and trap the steam, which gives me a steam facial.

Rebecca Dumas

7. A manicurist I know uses one to warm the lotion she massages into her clients' hands and arms.

Nancy Kelley, Orlando, FL

8. We used to use a slow cooker to keep damp towels warm for facials at the salon I worked at. Warm towels are great for all types of uses, even sore muscles!

Suzanne Steinbaecher, Lancaster, PA

9. I have a tiny one to keep oil warm for back rubs...very romantic.

Elf Noyes, Columbia, MO

Health

1. We make hot damp towels with large smooth stones in our slow cooker—it's a home, hot-stone massage!

Katherine Heldstab, Pittsburgh, PA

2. The massage place I go to uses a slow cooker to heat and keep her stones hot for hot stone massages, which are just to die for.

Cindy Carl, Barto, PA

3. When my husband hurt his shoulder, I kept a lavender and flaxseed hot pack in the slow cooker for his heat/ice therapy. The house smelled so nice!

Julie Bazata, Midway

4. When I was 28 years old, I developed Rheumatoid Arthritis. It attacks the joints and other systems of the body. It hit me hard and fast, and my hands were always swollen and hurting.

The only relief I had in the beginning was from my slow cooker filled with paraffin wax on low. I would dip my hands in repeatedly to build up a nice warm coating then cover them with plastic wrap and wrap my hands in bath towels. It was so comforting to get even temporary relief, and I could repeat the process as many times as needed.

I needed to buy a second crock pot so I had one to cook in.

Mary Ellen Stermer, Chemung, NY

5. The physical therapist used a slow cooker to warm up the paraffin she used on my arm when I was recovering from a broken arm.

Nancy Kelley, Orlando, FL

6. I kept warm, wet towels in my slow cooker when my husband had problems with his back. Instead of running up and down the stairs heating wash cloths in the microwave, I just put them in the slow cooker.

Cindy Mishou, Kingsburg, CA

7. I have a small cooker used for dips. I put water and mint in this when I had a cold, and inhaled the steam. I kept it covered between uses.

Kathy Thompson, Mount Vernon, OH

8. I have also put Vicks in a small slow cooker to help while a child was sick.

Adra Chim, Royse City, TX

9. Our midwife kept cloths warm in a slow cooker during the birth of our son. She filled it with water and herbs before adding the cloths.

Crystal Trost, Harrisonburg, VA

10. I and other nurses have used slow cookers to keep a supply of warm compresses available.

Maryella Vause, Blanco, TX

11. I've used slow cookers as humidifiers when camping in a cabin with electricity.

Elaine S. Good, Tiskilwa, IL

12. At the squad building we used a slow cooker to clean some oxygen masks by sterilizing them in it.

Lisa Seltzer, Riverside, NJ

Air Freshener

1. I have recreated the ambiance of the 90's potpourri craze by using my slow cooker to freshen and scent my home. If I'm using the slow cooker as an air freshener, I spray it first because vanilla, especially, forms a film on the crock that's hard to get off.

Susan Johnson, Minneapolis, MN

2. My aunt puts a cloves and water mixture in her slow cooker to remove the fish smell in her home after she cooks fish.

Deb Ward, Oxford, CT

3. I love to use my mini slow cooker for simmering potpourri. I slice a lemon and an orange with the rinds still on, add a tablespoon or two of whole cloves and several cinnamon sticks. I add water until the fruit is covered, then bring it to simmer with the lid on and then tilt the lid slightly to let the scent escape.

Dorthy Erlandson, Pullman, MI

4. I use my slow cooker to fill my house with the scent of the holiday seasons. I fill it half-full with hot water and add slices of oranges, lemons, cinnamon sticks, whole cloves, and whatever else I have on hand for a great holiday scent.

I used this also when showing our house when selling it. I could refrigerate the mixture and use it at least 1 or 2 times more.

Betty Detweiler, Centreville, MI

5. Make sure when using a slow cooker for a fragrance pot that the water doesn't evaporate.

Jane Emery, Noblesville, IN

Unplugged

1. I have a slow cooker that has 2 inserts, one metal, one stoneware. I took the metal insert, filled it with ice, set the stone insert in it and kept the potato salad cold. It totally worked, and everyone decided I was a genius.

Joy York, Wildwood, GA

2. Once we were at a ball game and saw one family used their slow cooker for a cooler. They just filled it with ice and set it on the table unplugged.

Colleen Van Dyke, New Holstein, WI

3. I bought a used slow cooker for my niece along with a kids' cookbook to inspire her to try out some recipes.

Unfortunately, the crock had a crack that had been repaired. Without knowing how they fixed it, we didn't want to use it because of the chemicals.

I plan on repurposing it as a planter, since it has a nice flower pattern on it.

Tracey Monroe, Madison, WI

4. After my first slow cooker stopped working, I used the crock as a flower pot.

Carmon Rye, Clifford, MI

5. I liked the idea for using the crock for an animal dish, because they can't dump it over.

Kathie Delano, Hebron, ME

6. We used the crock for a Halloween party for dunking apples.

Chris Lalonde, St. Clair Shores, MI

7. My grandmother used to use her old non-working slow cooker for her knitting yarn — she would feed the yarn through the vent hole on the lid and knit away. It kept the yarn from getting all twisted up.

Shenno Luia, Corinth, NY

8. One of my friends had this cute little container on the back of her kitchen sink filled with cooking utensils. Upon closer inspection, I noticed it was a 3-quart slow cooker. I asked her why she was using it like that, and she said because she didn't know what else to do with it because she didn't know how to use it.

She knows now. I bought her her first *Fix-It and Forget-It Cookbook*.

Tamie Jamison, Kennewick, WA

9. If I put hot water in my slow cooker, and do not even turn it on, it will still keep it nice and warm with the lid on. I can use this for cleaning or hot drinks.

Diana Franklin, Campbell, MO

Other Situations

1. If you use a slow cooker for something other than food, it is important to use that crock designated for non-food prep every time.

Tiffany Beka, Carlisle, PA

2. My brother uses his slow cooker to proof his bread dough. I got too lazy to make bread years ago.

Susan Johnson, Minneapolis, MN

3. We use our slow cooker to keep water hot to wash dishes with while camping.

Linda Spencer-Blackledge, Troutdale, OR

4. I use my slow cooker for heating water for dishes because we don't have a water heater right now.

Barbara A. Elliott, Osawtomie, KS

5. We used our slow cooker to keep water warm during an ice storm. The slow cookers use such a small amount of energy that they didn't tax our generator and we had a warm water supply for washing up.

Julie Bazata, Midway

6. For a wing eating event, I used 6 slow cookers to keep washcloths moist and warm for after the event.

Jeramy Lawrence, Aurora, CO

7. I think it's a nice touch to use a small slow cooker for small moist fingertip towels (that have been scented with something light and fresh, like Jean Nate) when you are serving barbecue, crab legs or any other food you eat with your fingers.

Yen Parrott, Houston, TX

8. At a picnic, a mom kept a slow cooker on warm with water in it and a few wash cloths for wiping messy hands and faces

Doreen Lappe, Carroll, IA

9. When I'm canning, I get water to boiling and put it in a preheated slow cooker with the lids and rings. This saves space on the stove when canning.

Candi Howman, Lewistown, MT

10. We used a slow cooker to keep a baby bottle warm while camping.

Jeramy Lawrence, Aurora, CO

11. We used slow cookers filled with water to warm bottles for infants at the preschool I worked at.

Jen Farrington, Shelburne, VT

12. We used our slow cooker for keeping towels warm for the birth of our puppies.

Mary Kruse, Kalispell, MT

13. Put water on the bottom of the slow cooker. Place coffee cups full of different colored chocolate pieces in the water. Turn on low to melt the chocolate and then use the chocolate to fill candy molds.

Jolene Wallace, San Antonio, TX

14. I've never tried it, but my nephew used one to clean paint off of kitchen cabinet handles.

Chris Jarrell, Mt. Morris, PA

15. I've used a slow cooker to clean wax off of candle holders.

C. Howe, Sunnyvale, CA

16. My mom cleaned old silverware in the slow cooker.

Jessica Casey, Sparks, NV

17. My husband and I make our own wine. We use the tiny little slow cooker, the one for dips, to melt the wax that the corked bottles are dipped in. My father-in-law does the same thing for his wines.

Rebekah Meyer, Caldwell, ID

18. At a dog show, someone kept their puppy's food warm in a slow cooker.

Cindy Mishou, Kingsburg, CA

19. I once hid Easter candy and toys in the cold slow cooker as I knew my daughter would not look there.

Eileen Marsh, Anamosa, IA

Storage and Cleaning

Places to Keep Slow Cookers

1. My slow cooker is always on the counter—that is how much we use it.
Amy Freeman Marquez, Brevard, NC

2. I am so excited about my new slow cooker! I think I may leave it on the kitchen counter. I hope this will inspire me to try lots of new recipes. Whenever I need to free up the space in my small kitchen, I will probably have to move it into the dining room—temporarily, of course.
Karen Arn, Helena, AL

3. I store my prettiest slow cooker on my kitchen counter, since I use it several times a week, and want to keep it handy. The cheerful design of cherries on the slow cooker adds charm to my kitchen's decor.
Cathy Fraser, Albuquerque, NM

4. One slow cooker is under the kitchen sink, the other is on the counter.
Paula Lewis, Poland, OH

5. Usually one slow cooker is on my counter, one is on top of my refrigerator and another in a cabinet.

Susan Valley-Putt, Allegany, NY

6. I have a ledge above the cupboards and I have all my slow cookers lined up there.

Rebecca Dumas

7. I put my slow cookers back in their boxes and store them in a closet.

Debbie Caraballo, Manahawkin, NJ

8. I have a coat closet that I converted to an appliance pantry where I keep my slow cooker.

Christine Ranallo, Medina, NY

9. I have a closet in my dining room where I keep all my slow cookers.

Tina Schwab, South Attleboro, MA

10. My husband built out a hall coat closet for me to store my slow cookers in and it works.

Molly Garza, Katy, TX

11. I keep the boxes so I can store extra slow cookers in the basement. I keep the one I use the most on a shelf in kitchen.

Karen Gaines, Cincinnati, OH

12. I keep my slow cooker under my bed because I have an apartment and not much storage space.

Sheila J. Moline, Reno, NV

13. I keep my slow cookers in the garage.

Rose Simmons, Grand Prairie, TX

153

14. I have a very small kitchen and very little counter space, so I can't leave my slow cooker out on the counter when it is not in use. I keep my slow cooker, and all my other small appliances, in boxes in the garage.

Carol Mathay, Shoreline, WA

15. I have a large shelving unit in my basement just for slow cookers, large griddles, roasting pans, and large serving platters.

Edward Engelman, Menasha, WI

16. I actually had a built-in cabinet made with closed storage in the bottom for my slow cookers. The top has glass doors where I display antique dishes owned by my grandmothers and my mother.

Martha Deaton, Fulton, MS

17. I have a shelf for my slow cookers in my pantry, out in the open, so I need to keep it clean and attractive.

Marlene Graber, Sparta, WI

18. I keep my slow cookers in one of my under-counter pull-out drawers: handy but out of sight.

Cherry Smith, El Paso, TX

19. I keep my slow cookers on a shelf next to the kitchen so they are out of the way but still easy to access.

Sharon Yoder, Doylestown, PA

20. I keep my slow cookers on a shelf in the mud/laundry room as I don't have room in the kitchen for these multiple large items.

Beverly Cowdery, Freeman, VA

21. I have a special pull-out shelf that is built just for my slow cooker.

Beverly Wallace, New Hudson, MI

Ways to Store Them

1. I keep my slow cooker at easy access because if it is hard to get to, I will not think to use it.
   Stephanie Ringler, Weston, OH

2. When I'm storing my slow cookers, I put the cord doubled through the handle on the lid and pull the plug through the resulting loop. That way the cord doesn't get stuck or smack me in the face as I lift it down.
   Linda Spencer-Blackledge, Troutdale, OR

3. Don't keep your slow cooker packed away; keep it within easy reach. You will be inclined to use it more.
   June S. Groff, Denver, PA

4. If not kept in a box, an old pillowcase can keep slow cookers dust-free.
   Kathy Thompson, Mount Vernon, OH

5. I wrap my slow cooker in a clear plastic bag (the kind that fit a small trash can) to keep out the dust.
   Karen Mulhollem, Ocala, FL

Methods of Cleaning

1. I clean the crock with a damp sponge and Brillo pad. Then I rinse it with a paper towel and dry.
   Norma Pratt, Brighton, Ontario

2. I use a damp cloth on my slow cooker, and I am a stickler for keeping it clean during cooking.
   Molly Garza, Katy, TX

3. Clean out any odors and stains with a mixture of cream of tartar and water. Rub it on, and let that sit, then wipe it out.

Bonnie Anderson, Simpsonville, SC

4. I just clean the outside with a SOS pad. I never clean inside the metal electrical unit.

Frances Raabe, Seattle, WA

5. Mr. Clean Magic Eraser Bars are perfect for cleaning the electrical unit!

Jeanne Caia, Ontario, NY

6. When I burn something that sticks and won't come out, and no scrubbing, scraping, soaking or scratching will get it out, what do I do? I use baking soda and vinegar!
Sometimes it takes days of constantly treating it, but it will all finally come out.

Mrs. Darcy Castle, Clio, MI

7. I have an electric stovetop and one day I tried my stovetop cleaner on my slow cooker and ta da! That's what I always use now with paper towels.

Rebecca Dumas

8. I spray my slow cooker crock with cooking spray. However, if food does stick on, I soak it in water and baking soda for at least an hour and the burned-on part will come off much easier.

Carna Reitz, Remington, VA

9. I use a very warm wet washcloth on my slow cooker. I use vinegar, if needed, for stubborn stuck-on food.

Angela Smith, Glenwood City, WI

10. I just wipe the electrical unit with a damp cloth soon after cooking before the food dries on.

Eve Mercer, Hebron, ND

11. After removing food from my slow cooker, I immediately fill the crock with hot soapy water. I've never had anything stick!

Cathy Hoyt, Moyock, NC

12. After using and storing leftovers, I always fill the crock with hot water, a squirt of dish soap, and turn it on high for an hour. I can almost always just wipe the crock clean.

Karen Schulz, Janesville, WI

13. I rub the crock gently with a damp cloth. For stuck-on stuff, I use Bon Ami.

Robin Gilliam, Puyallup, WA

14. I use a warm damp rag and elbow grease.

Bernadette Smith, Hibbing, MN

Baking in the Slow Cooker

1. I grease the baking insert or can with solid vegetable shortening and fill the insert or can only half-full to allow for rising.

   Heat needs to be able to circulate around the insert, so if a baking rack isn't available, I crumple up enough aluminum foil to raise the can about an inch from the bottom of the crock.

   If you don't have a lid, cover the can with a double thickness of paper towels.

   Molly Garza, Katy, TX

2. When baking my meatloaf in a foil pan, I cut holes in the bottom and sides so that the fat runs off while cooking.

   Jeanne Caia, Ontario, NY

3. I wish I had a bread pan for my slow cooker. I love baking, especially sweet breads like banana breads and zucchini bread.

   If I had this accessory I would not have to plan half my day around baking bread as I know the slow cooker accessory would make it a more time efficient process that I would be able to do even on days that I am at work.

   Noel Bigelow, Bellefontaine, OH

7. I don't double cakes or stuffing/dressing. The sides get too thick and brown, while the middle needs more time.

Marlene Graber, Sparta, WI

8. When I make a cake, a meatloaf or something else for which I don't want the excess water accumulating in the slow cooker, I use a double layer of paper towel under the lid to absorb the liquid before it gets to my food.

Donna Davis, Horse Cave, KY

4. A friend of mine made a chocolate cake in a slow cooker. While it wasn't the prettiest cake, it was moist and stayed warm, perfect to serve ice cream over.

Noel Bigelow, Bellefontaine, OH

5. I particularly love those chocolate saucy cakes that bake in the slow cooker and create their own sauce. Served over ice cream, they are an easy and elegant dessert.

Karen Sauder, Adamstown, PA

9. A paper towel on top, just under the lid helps collect condensation when the lid is lifted. I am careful when lifting the lid to tilt it when it's not over the slow cooker, lest the condensation drip back into the crock.

Kelley Millemon, Alton, IL

6. I made a turtle cheesecake in the slow cooker. It turned out perfectly and there were no cracks as can sometimes happen with the oven method.

Elaine Jones, Grand Rivers, KY

10. I have never bought baking inserts. I sometimes use a smaller casserole dish, bread pan, or vegetable steamer in my slow cooker.

Martha Deaton, Fulton, MS

11. I have steamed my Christmas pudding in soup cans when I wanted to make multiples for gifts.

Sandy Olson, Turton, SD

12. I've placed an upside-down saucer in the bottom of my crock and set a coffee can on it for making brown bread and plum puddings.

Jean Moulton, Windsor, ME

13. I don't have an actual baking insert, but I make do with what I have. I just set a bread loaf pan on empty tuna cans.

Karen Schulz, Janesville, WI

14. It's best if the baking insert doesn't touch the bottom so the steam can get all the way around it.

Jean Moulton, Windsor, ME

15. I use my pan directly in the crock of my slow cooker.

Kelley Millemon, Alton, IL

16. I've put a casserole dish in the slow cooker which I set on canning jar lids.

Crystal Trost, Harrisonburg, VA

17. I would like a trivet to put under my small spring-form pan. I always just crumple some foil to put under it, but a trivet would be less wasteful.

Jill Brock, Rochester, NY

18. I have used a small rack that I found fit into one of my cookers. I used small glass bowls or baking dishes that I found in my cupboards that would fit.

Betty Detweiler, Centreville, MI

19. I put waxed paper in the bottom of the crock before I put in the batter if I want the baking to come out in one piece.

Grease the bottom of the crock, put in the waxed paper, and grease that, just like a cake pan.

Sharen Wittrock, Sheboygan, WI

20. Don't lift the lid to peek, because it breaks the seal that is caused by the steam.

Beverly Cowdery, Freeman, VA

21. To keep the lid on my slow cooker, I keep my husband out of the kitchen.

Marianne White, Aberdeen, MD

22. Try it out before you bake something in your slow cooker for public consumption! Sometimes it just *does not* work well.

Karen Schulz, Janesville, WI

Transporting Slow Cookers

Keeping the Lid On

1. I tie the lid down with fabric, wrap the slow cooker in a towel, and then set it in a box.

   Lynn Brokaw, Alamosa, CO

2. I put tin foil between the crock and the lid, rubber band the lid to the handles, and place the cooker into a tight-fitting cardboard box on the floor of the car.

   Jeanne Caia, Ontario, NY

3. I put painter's tape all the way around the lid.

   Arlene Hall, Houston, PA

4. My husband runs a bungee cord around the electrical unit and through the handle on the lid.

   Or I'll use two cords to tie up the slow cooker like a package (front to back, and side to side) if the handle is a knob.

   Then I put the slow cooker in a plastic garbage bag and place it inside a cooler with wheels and a pull handle. This contains any spills and makes hauling everything into the office a breeze.

   Becky Thompson, San Antonio, TX

5. A nylon luggage strap with a buckle works to keep the lid secure when I take my cooker somewhere.
Michael Feight, Eau Claire, WI

6. I use a bungee strap to secure the crock and lid.
Mary Ellen Stermer, Chemung, NY

7. Fasten the lid with a piece of elastic tied in a loop so that it can function as a rubber band would without melting. Do not overfill, and remove some food to another container for transport if needed.
Beth Bigler, Lancaster, PA

8. I put a hot pad on the lid of the slow cooker and place a thick rubber band over the top with the band under each handle.
Deb Slater, Stilwell, KS

9. I turn the lid upside down when I'm transporting my full slow cooker.
Barbara Yoder, Christiana, PA

Carrying Containers

1. We always set the slow cooker in a cooler of some kind so that it fits snug, and any spills are contained.
Janet Peterson, Pierz, MN

2. Laundry baskets with towels in the bottom are great for stabilizing slow cookers in the car, and two large rubber bands work great for securing the lids. I use rubber bands from asparagus bunches I get from the warehouse stores.
Alexis Roy, Sauk Rapids, MN

3. I use an apple box that I get from the grocer to carry my slow cooker. They are deep, well-built, and have handles.

Laurie Gunter, Woodbury, MN

4. When transporting my slow cooker, I don't make stuff that will slosh. I put my slow cooker into a box and wrap towels around it which also keeps the heat in.

Frances Raabe, Seattle, WA

5. I wrap my slow cooker in a towel and put it in a cardboard box that is just the right size. I wrote "Crock Pot Box" on the side so it doesn't get thrown away.

Jane Curtis, Fremont, MI

6. I have a hand-made wooden crate that my slow cooker fits into. I just pick it up and go!

Sharon Miller, Holmesville, OH

7. I like to put foil on the top of the crock, then the lid, and then I use rubber bands to keep the lid in place. I place it in a towel-lined box if it's already heated up. Sometimes I will place a large garbage bag in the box first for spill protection. Finally, I cover it with another large towel to keep the heat in.

Sue Smith-McClain, Brookfield, WI

8. I have an insulated carrying bag from a previous slow cooker that I use, which zips around the top and helps to hold the lid in place. Then, I wrap a large bath towel around the whole thing and set it into a cardboard box and then put it in the car. If I do have a spill, the towel will usually absorb it and keep it from soiling the interior of my car. The cardboard box adds another layer of spill-catching, plus a flat bottom helps it to ride better, too.

Angel Barnes, Kinderhook, IL

9. If I'm using the smaller slow cookers and transporting them, I place them in a plastic grocery bag and tie the bag handles down tight over the lid. Then I place the cooker in one of my reusable grocery bags.

Cherry Smith, El Paso, TX

10. I use a large baking sheet to keep the slow cooker stable, place foil over the food but under the lid, and strap down the lid with twine if I'm concerned about it coming off.

I place a large towel over it to keep it warm and secure.

Alys Corbin, Brick, NJ

11. I have a tote made for slow cookers that I bought at a craft fair. It's quilted, plus I use a towel to line the inside for those just-in-case moments I might have.

Nancy Thackston, Gadsden, AL

12. I carry my slow cooker in a casserole carrier.

Donna Vail, Golconda, IL

13. I am a quilter, so I made a carry case with a drawstring top to keep the lid in place while traveling. It also insulates the cooker to stay hot on the inside without burning me, like a large hotpad to cover my cooker.

Melinda Myers, Mount Joy, PA

In the Vehicle

1. I make sure I drive when I've got a full slow cooker in the car!

Pauline Crawford, Yamhill, OR

2. I set the slow cooker on the floor of the car, usually wedged between the seats, or I buckle it in with the seat belt on the seat!

Barbara A. Elliott, Osawtomie, KS

3. Secure the top! I once spilled potato corn chowder in my car and it smelled like sour milk for months no matter what I did.

Mary Ellen Stermer, Chemung, NY

4. Place non-skid material, such as a shelf-liner, in the trunk, then a cookie sheet or baking pan, then non-skid material (like the rubber shelf liner), and finally the slow cooker.

Marie McFadden, Clover, SC

What Else to Take Along

1. Take a couple of dish towels to clean the outside before serving (just in case it sloshed during transport).

Patty Paulsen, South Jordan, UT

2. Take the ingredients in separate closed containers and add them to the slow cooker when you arrive at your destination.

Chris Maestes, McGill, NV

3. I wrap up my slow cooker in old towels. I keep old towels for that reason in one of my kitchen cabinets.

Jean McDowell, Duncan, OK

Other Considerations

1. Don't overfill your cooker when you need to transport it. If mine is overfull, I use a tea pitcher to transport things like chili or soups.

Amy Freeman Marquez, Brevard, NC

2. I have seen friends put the food in another container for transport, then put it back into the slow cooker when they get to where they are going.

Amanda Payne, Pilot Mountain, NC

3. I use slow cooker liners and loosely tie the top of the liner closed until I reach my destination.

Kathie High, Lititz, PA

4. I roasted a turkey to take to a family holiday gathering a few years ago. I used my slow cooker to transport it the 75 miles from my house to the gathering. The slow cooker kept it warm the whole way without being plugged in.

Angel Barnes, Kinderhook, IL

Serving

1. I lay criss-crossed strips of foil down one side over the the bottom and up the other side so they hang over the edge.

   When the cooking is done, I grab the foil strip ends and use them like handles to lift out the food.
   Arlene Hall, Houston, PA

2. Make a foil basket to get solid things like lasagna out in one piece.
   Shelby Sill, Dallas, TX

3. I lay a strip of parchment paper, wax paper or foil under the meatloaf lengthwise as well as crosswise in order to remove it whole.
   Julie Bazata

4. I use turkey lifters to get meat loaves, cakes and lasagna out of my slow cooker.
   Janie Lindsay, Silver Lake, OH

5. For a whole chicken, I slip a large cutlery fork in the cavity, and use my extra large lifting spatula to remove the bird whole and undisturbed. I use a syringe for removing the clear juices to make gravy or au jus.
   Laurie Gunter, Woodbury, MN

6. I cut the lasagna or meat loaf in half and use a wide spatula to lift out each half.
   Marlene Graber, Sparta, WI

7. I use a plastic slow cooker bag to get food out in one piece. I lift out the plastic liner and move the food onto a platter.

Nancy Robb, Cadillac, MI

8. The only cake I've made in the slow cooker is dump cake which gets served with a large spoon. I treat lasagna the same way.

Mollie Dosch, Oceanside, CA

9. I serve from the slow cooker directly.

Paula Byers, Marietta, OH

10. Wait until the slow cooker cools. Refrigerate the crock overnight, and the food comes out beautifully the next day.

Mollie Dosch, Oceanside, CA

11. I don't always take food out of the slow cooker to serve it. I just take the crock from the electrical unit to the table because they're very attractive nowadays.

Pat Luey, Yelm, WA

We include tips from various viewpoints so you can make your own fully-informed decision. For example, cooks differ on how to serve slow-cooked food. Think of this book as a circle of cooks, discussing their experiences and preferences. We hope you benefit from all of that as you decide how to proceed.

12. Take the finished food out of the slow cooker for serving. Garnish with something green when possible.

Jan Mast, Lancaster, PA

13. Lasagna and pasta dishes we serve directly out of the slow cooker. Forget about pretty square pieces of lasagna — it is considered more casserole-style when it comes out of the slow cooker.

Sheryl Rogener, Tracy, CA

14. I use a slotted spoon to remove the larger pieces of food. Then I place a container in the sink and pour out the juices. The sink makes pouring easier because

it is lower. Plus, if anything spills, it is in the sink!

June S. Groff, Denver, PA

15. Slow cookers are great for serving and keeping food warm as a buffet. Much better than using hot water baths with a sterno burner which always seem to need watching!

Jean Robinson, Pemberton, NJ

16. An extra pair of hands is helpful. I have someone lift out the ceramic crock and tilt it while I remove the food.

Alys Corbin, Brick, NJ

17. If the crock was sprayed before I started cooking, I turn it upside down over a plate or platter to get the food out.

Jean Moulton, Windsor, ME

18. I don't just put a slow cooker out—I make an interesting presentation around it. I use Christmas decorations, for example. If I am using the cooker for mulling scents, I place some clove-studded fruit around

it. If the slow cooker is holding a dessert, I try to have some of the ingredients, like shaved chocolate and raspberries, laying around it.

Molly Garza, Katy, TX

19. Buy a silicone knife for cutting lasagna so that you don't scratch the ceramic crock.

Patricia Slattery, Hopewell Junction, NY

20. Always use plastic utensils or wooden spoons in the slow cooker crock. Metal scratches.

Kathie Delano, Hebron, ME

21. I cut a small slit in the paper tablecloth where I will be placing the cooker to serve food, and then I feed the cord through the slit to keep it out of sight.

June S. Groff, Denver, PA

Index

INDEX OF TOPICS

INDEX OF TOPICS

INDEX OF TOPICS

About the Authors

Phyllis Pellman Good is a *New York Times* bestselling author whose books have sold more than 12 million copies.

Good is the author of the nationally acclaimed *Fix-It and Forget-It* slow-cooker cookbooks, several of which have appeared on *The New York Times* bestseller list, as well as the bestseller lists of *USA Today, Publishers Weekly,* and *Book Sense.*

The series includes:

- *Fix-It and Forget-It Cookbook (Revised and Updated): 700 Great Slow-Cooker Recipes*
- *Fix-It and Forget-It Lightly (Revised and Updated): Healthy, Low-Fat Recipes for Your Slow Cooker*
- *Fix-It and Forget-It 5-Ingredient Favorites: Comforting Slow-Cooker Recipes*
- *Fix-It and Forget-It Christmas Cookbook: 600 Slow-Cooker Holiday Recipes*
- *Fix-It and Forget-It Diabetic Cookbook: Slow Cooker Favorites to Include Everyone* (with the American Diabetes Association)
- *Fix-It and Forget-It Vegetarian Cookbook: 565 Delicious Slow-Cooker, Stove-Top, Oven, and Salad Recipes, plus 50 Suggested Menus*
- *Fix-It and Forget-It PINK Cookbook: More Than 700 Great Slow-Cooker Recipes!*

Good is also the author of the *Fix-It and Enjoy-It* series (featuring stove-top and oven recipes), a "cousin" series to the phenomenally successful *Fix-It and Forget-It* cookbooks.

Nearly all of the Tips in this book have come from the friends of the *Fix-It and Forget-It* cookbooks—including our faithful recipe contributors from all over North America, followers of our Fix-It and Forget-It blog (fix-itandforget-it.com), and hundreds of thousands of our social media friends.

Join us on Facebook at www.facebook.com/fixitandforgetit
You can also find us on Twitter: @FixItForgetIt
Look for us, too, on Pinterest.